To Bob
with love —
Grace
, 1947

SOME
DAYS
WERE
HAPPY

SOME

DAYS

WERE

HAPPY

By LOUIS SOBOL

Foreword by GENE FOWLER

RANDOM HOUSE NEW YORK

FIRST PRINTING

A few items in this book appeared originally in the *New York Journal-American*. Acknowledgment is here made for their use.

Published in New York by Random House, Inc.,
and simultaneously in Toronto, Canada,
by Random House of Canada, Ltd., 1947.
Manufactured in the United States of America
By The Haddon Craftsmen, Inc., Scranton, Pa.

Designed by Meyer Wagman

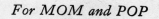

For MOM and POP

For MOM and POP

CONTENTS

FOREWORD

by

GENE FOWLER

Spring came to New York like a hard-to-get woman suddenly yielding, and with it came the galley-proofs of Louis Sobol's book. Both events were heartening and complete, and shining with gay surprise.

Just why anyone should find astonishment in a New York spring or in Sobol is a matter for the psychoanalysts to ponder. Both the season and the man have been making the rounds for some years, and we should be quite used to them by now. Still, when buds and leaves come to the trees of Central Park at a time when men in the tall towers downtown speak of world panic, and when Sobol writes of his own Valentine boyhood while almost all the other authors are furiously scratching at the fur of the great Red Bear, we are allowed to smile again.

It may be said of Sobol, as it has been of Maugham, that he brings no message of this puzzling day. Long ago, Ring Lardner said to some of his pals that he himself fought shy of messages, adding, "Why should I attempt something that Western Union does better for a fee of sixty cents?"

To avoid new blows upon my hoary head (and you are

at liberty to make a pun here) for an unjust inference that I am opposed to writers of sincere messages, permit me to say that we need fair and honest interpretations of the world scene. But, sir and madam, if you please, I have no stomach for the bedlam shrieks of radio hacks and the endless droolings of the self-anointed literati who swing dead cats on every page and ask me to believe that they are slaying tigers and vile leopards.

Sobol does have a message, if you will, and it is implied rather than howled out from the crow's-nest. It is a reassurance that life was young, still is young, and ever will be deep in the American solar plexus. His manner and his way are neither blatant nor pugnacious. His modesty and his decency should not be mistaken for the badges of weakness. After all, that most amiable of men, Jack Dempsey, does not walk along Broadway slugging citizens on their chins. And who would deny that the mightiest champion of our time lacks power or courage?

* * *

Until reading Sobol's book of his Connecticut boyhood, I always had thought that newspaper columnists were born old men. Else how could they see everything, know everything, and (the reverse of the fabulous trio of simians) tell everything? Indeed, I had imagined that the columnist was born at, say, eighty-six, and progressively grew younger. He descended from senility, shedding his years, as it were, until he came to puberty; then, after a fine tussle with names and pranks of celebrities, his dying words were not "Da! Da!" but "Toots Shor" or "Billingsley."

To come upon a book written by a Broadway columnist, and—wonder of wonders!—published by that cosmopolite, the gifted raconteur, Mr. Bennett Cerf, and edited by that literary Simon Legree, Mr. Saxe Commins, and to find

that the book has to do with the springtime of Louis Sobol
—well, gossip, it is as reassuring as the light shed by
Portia's candle.

To me Sobol always has seemed the real successor to
our good friend, the late O. O. McIntyre. Odd McIntyre
wrote of a New York that was real only in the minds of
the out-of-towners. The good and kindly McIntyre would
sit in his apartment at the Ritz, or perhaps stroll with his
dog on the Avenue, dreaming up stories of "furtive figures
in Pell Street doorways," and "small old women selling
nosegays on the Bowery."

McIntyre, insofar as I can remember, never attacked
nor did anyone a bad turn. Still, his articles on New York
make it appear to dwellers elsewhere that they were fortunate indeed never to have seen beyond their own hay-
stacks the evils of the city of sin and perdition.

Sobol, however, differs from McIntyre in that in his
column he chronicles the New York scene as it is—not as
it appears in the dreams of those who never have partaken
of its excitements. With all his charm and goodness of
heart, McIntyre's New York was as different from Sobol's
as is the stage Irishman or Jew from the real McCoy or
the actual Nussbaum.

*   *   *

When you read the pages that follow this inadequate
introduction by an old reporter, may you live again your
own youth, whether in Sobol's Connecticut or in Gene
Buck's Michigan or Ben Hecht's Illinois or John Doe's
Florida.

The old iron stove in the Sobol household, Mom's teapot bank, the streets that are all-American: Congress
Avenue, Church, Chapel; Pa's hobby of collecting crockery shards; the piano lessons, the tragedies of a world-in-

little, the courtships, the early days in the newspaper business . . . It is a catalogue of the warm things in life.

In one of the several interludes that appear between the chapters of this book, Sobol says, *"Reluctantly I left. You can't stay with the past too long."*

Still, the past is a true possession, untaxable, irrevocable —and no one can take it from us.

New York
April, 1947

SOME

DAYS

WERE

HAPPY

CHAPTER ONE

The Kitchen Stove

Life in our home, as I remember it, frolicked or brooded around the kitchen stove. There the family gathered for food, for warmth, for entertainment, for reminiscence, for study and for solace. It was the meeting place and the capitol of our little community; it was our council chamber, theatre, lecture hall and altar. We settled disputes there, acted out our comedies, wept dramatically, debated issues of the day and worshipped near it as if it were a sacred shrine.

What a stove that was! Its ebony coat glistened with daily polishings and its filigreed nickel trimmings were rubbed to an image-giving sheen. On its oven door was embossed the proud name "Monarch" in bold, imperial letters. Its stovepipe rose from somewhere in its rear toward a brass-encircled hole in the chimney. Half way up was a damper, with a twisted-wire handle whose mysterious function only the older folks ever knew. Directly above it was a shelf in glossy nickel on which pans of newly baked bread and cookies were arrayed with military precision, their wire handles as if in salute.

The kitchen was no cubicle for a cook with claustrophobia. It was the largest and most important room in the house. There were other constellations besides that iron-and-nickel sun in our little universe; there was a large, square table of oak at which we ate all our meals; there were chairs of unmatched design and unequal sturdiness. There was a pantry with dishes, handpainted and unadorned, cups with ears missing and one master mug marked with glittering letters "Father," bowls and tureens, glasses plain and some which were then called "cut" and therefore the last word in elegance. The icebox was a two-tiered hulk with a protruding brass spigot for draining off sawdust-flecked ice water. Our kitchen was indeed best described by a word too frequently used for other purposes; it was homely.

No article of furniture ever supplanted the kitchen stove in our affections. In sub-zero weather we of the up-and-coming generation sat snug up against it and read Henty, Oliver Optic, Horatio Alger, Jr., Burt L. Standish, Nick Carter, Ralph Henry Barbour, Dickens, Kipling and other less-loved and now-forgotten authors whose names appeared in our school books while we toasted our stockinged feet in the open oven of our "Monarch" and our pride.

Most of the houses in our small-town neighborhood boasted furnaces which tried to distribute heat evenly and amply throughout the frame structures. In those long blizzardy Connecticut winters, these cellar monsters wasted their fiery breath in their deep-bellied grates and sent only tepid puffs of air to the remote outposts of parlor and bedrooms. To stand over one of the registers and feel a faint current of heat only as far up as the knees was more titillating than comforting. Only in the immediate vicinity of our "Monarch" was any real and soul-satisfying warmth to be found.

4

Usually the big aluminum tea kettle danced on one of the cast-iron lids and sang as its spout joyously waved plumes of steam. My mother and father were chain tea drinkers. An earthenware pot in which the leaves were always being steeped was a constant companion-piece to the kettle.

The stove handle with its graceful steel spiral was warm to the touch and its permanent place was in one of the rear, cooler disks. One of its frequent uses was to push orange peels closer and closer to the hottest lids. There they shrivelled gradually and sent forth a heavenly aroma. The golden orange changed to rust by the intense heat, then became coffee-brown and finally stiffened into a crisp of charcoal.

Another diverting pastime—one which drew the stern disapproval of my mother—was to place a lump of sugar on the stove and watch it flame up for a second before melting into a brown, coagulated mound. The blob of melted sugar sent a noxiously sweet odor through the whole house and ruined the high polish achieved by Mother's relentless rubbing. To her there was no greater mortification than to have a stranger fix his glance on the spot on the stove's surface which marked our crime.

On the rare occasions when Father and Mother left our house to visit relatives, we children were given elaborate instructions on the operation of the damper. We were cautioned to turn the handle until it was horizontal if the stove glowed to redness, to vertical if the fire showed signs of smoldering, and at an angle for a half draft. These instructions succeeded only in bewildering me, and all my manipulations of the damper were strictly experimental. I knew enough to add a few coals from the black scuttle that always stood, half full, under the iron apron in front of the stove, but whether I should turn the damper up or down or sideways when replenishing the fire remained an unsolved mystery to me. Trial and error was my only method.

My sister and I, left to our own devices, played with fire—and were not burned. We would let the coals in the grate flame until the lids blushed mildly and then became a frightening crimson. At this point they seemed almost transparent. It was fun to drop bread crumbs and watch them stiffen, sparkle, and then wither. Oak leaves from the back yard turned into somber colors and then shrivelled as if in agony. Water, a drop at a time, danced a brief crazy pirouette before going up in a tiny puff of steam. By the time our parents came back the fire needed desperate measures for revival and the surface of the stove a new coat of "Black Cat" polish.

Of course we had no servants. My mother did all the housework herself. She swept and dusted every room, washed and dried the dishes, with occasional assistance from my father, beat the carpets, scoured the pots and pans, baked and roasted and stewed, preserved fruits in the summer and knitted and mended in the winter, shopped and bargained, guarded our finances and nursed us through illness, was the confidante and confessor and counselor, the court of last appeal, the law, the book, the word. Mother was everything because she never asked anything.

She prepared the breakfast and the noon-day dinner and the six o'clock supper, and it was she who served us. We children were too young to help, but my father would lend a hand with the clearing of the table and the washing of the dishes after the night meal, singing out in his fine baritone a medley of his favorites, usually the melancholy, "Just Break the News to Mother" and the gayer,

"Where Did You Get That Hat—Oh You Lucky Fellow."

Then Mama would settle down in the rocker near the stove and read a paper or knit. Shortly thereafter Papa would move a chair over to the front of the stove to read his part of the paper. My sister, Janet, aloof to the beckoning allurement of the stove, would sit at the kitchen table reading her primer or playing a game.

About 9 o'clock, my father would stir the coals with the poker and that was the signal that it was bedtime. On Saturday nights, the curfew was extended to perhaps as late as 10 o'clock.

Mother and Father would rise at 5:30 in the morning, so that by 7 o'clock, when we were awakened, the kitchen stove was aglow and doing heavy duty under its burden of pots and pans and kettles. Breakfast always began with a dish of prunes with a few lemon peels floating in the juice. Steaming oatmeal in a sea of milk followed and then came a cup of rich cocoa. There were great heaps of black bread and a hillock of sweet butter and jars of Mother's home-made jam and jellies. We left the kitchen for school prepared for a half day of famine. Sometimes, just before we were sent off to school, one of us would open the oven door to see if Ma were baking a cake or making some of her tiny, prune-stuffed puddings.

Usually Ma was.

Teapot Treasury

In our circle no one operated the complicated machinery of a home under a budget. Our economic system had the virtue of simplicity. We knew there were purchases to be made daily and bills to meet at the end of the week. When my father deposited his pay envelope on the kitchen table with a mock-modest shyness, every penny had been allocated by our Lord High Chancellor of the Exchequer—Mother. There were always the grocer, butcher, milkman to take care of weekly, the rent and the coal bills monthly—and always and inescapably the installment collector. In a separate category were the quarters set aside for the gas meter.

My mother's budgetary system was sound and effective. She belonged to that school of economists whose faith was in the teapot-and-small-vase doctrine. She managed to scrimp a penny here, a dime there, and even a dollar now and then, and tuck these accruals away in an old teapot. Kept high on a kitchen shelf, side by side with a half dozen vases which secreted coins of all denominations, the teapot, because it was even out of Mother's reach, seemed to her completely burglar-proof. When the milkman came, it was a simple matter to step up on a kitchen chair and reach for the copper and silver treasury. The newsboy was paid out of a vase with a faded rose design and the landlord's monthly demand was met out of a bowl-like affair guarded on its surface by two fierce dragons who were more intent upon chasing each other than on their responsibility for the cache. If a vandal did appear, my childish wonder was as to how the monsters would ever disengage the knot into which their tails were tied around the handle of the vase.

Another receptacle was set apart exclusively for the quarters which were used in the gas meter, but the prize treasure-trove was the teapot. It was the great open secret of our home. My mother, I am sure, believed that it was invisible to our eyes. We never hinted that we could see it, in spite of its prominence among the vases on the shelf.

When the teapot was so full that the lid would no longer fit, she would shoo us out of the kitchen and have us wait outside until she gave the signal. We trooped in and acted out great expectancy as best we could. Mother stood by the table and looked down at the bulge under her apron.

"Well, sit down, sit down," she commanded. "I never saw such people—they don't want to sit."

That was the cue to take our places around the table and wait for her to lift the curtain of her apron to let her little show go on. The battered old teapot was brought out with a flourish.

"Hmmmm," my father would grunt, in mock disappointment, "I thought maybe a pigeon. I like magicians with pigeons—not with old junk."

My mother would throw him a scornful glance and reply, "This is a pigeon, too. It lays golden eggs."

This playful colloquy rarely varied. Father seldom changed his gambit and Mother knew her line by heart.

The next gesture was to empty the contents of the teapot on the red-checkered oilcloth which covered the table, and a cascade of pennies, nickels, dimes and quarters rolled out. There were always one or two dollar bills. Now came the stacking of the various denominations and the counting of the hoard. In the meantime, Mother offered a running commentary on how she accumulated these savings. Two cents by her choice of one bunch of radishes over another; four cents by shopping from store to store for potatoes; a nickel by walking instead of taking the trolley car; fifteen cents by taking a lesser-known brand of flour. With glee she repeated a sentiment much quoted at the time: "Every little bit added to what you got makes just a little bit more."

Papa would shake his head and mumble, "I'm not so sure. Nowadays, banks are a little safer. I read in the paper there was a robbery over at Lundson's. Someone just walked in, opened the cash drawer, helped himself, and, whisht, he was gone."

"No one would ever think of looking in an old teapot," was Mother's defense.

"Oh, no," Papa guffawed. "They'd look under your mattress."

That was the signal for all of us to giggle. It was the better part of wisdom to laugh at Father's jokes.

Then came the animated debate as to what we could do with this fabulous wealth. My father voted for a much-needed winter coat for Mother. Mama overruled that motion. She wanted the money for shoes for the children and a hat for Father. A compromise was effected usually. In one instance that compromise took the form of a beautiful plaster statuette depicting Custer's last stand. It showed the General standing defiantly against Indians in the imagined distance while he supported the two wounded soldiers who clung to him. On another occasion it was a mute and inglorious canary in a gilded cage, and still another, a set for burning artistic designs by needle-point into the stenciled pieces of wood and leather which came with the package. For years our house harbored relics of Mother's parsimony and extravagance.

In our gentle neighborhood, no one fretted too much about whether the portals to our snug little homes were securely locked at night. We trusted each other. We were only casually shocked by the robberies and hold-ups reported by our newspaper because the crimes were always committed somewhere else—usually in the bigger cities.

But one day, Mrs. Casey's house was robbed. Mrs. Casey was a widow who lived half way down the block. Two days later, we learned that the Stroebes, only two doors away, had been burglarized. The thief had taken a squirrel-fur neckpiece and four bronze candlesticks from

Mrs. Casey's home, but at Stroebe's, it was evident he had proceeded more leisurely, for he had gone off with Mr. Stroebe's best suit, two hats, Mrs. Stroebe's silver platter and a big clock whose works were framed in glass.

Naturally, the whole neighborhood was alarmed. It was quite exciting to us younger ones. A big heavy-set man came around one day and asked a great many questions. Joe Joneson, who had been the lone patrol in our section for years, now had a companion cop on the beat. The newspapers fussed a great deal right on the front pages about this crime wave in a peaceful community and directed leading questions in big type at our embarrassed superintendent of police.

There were no more robberies, but Mama was worried about her little hideaway banks and for days there were whispered huddles between her and my father, but no decision was ever reached.

Then word came that the thief had been nabbed by the police. Poor old Joe Joneson was bitterly disappointed, for he had hoped to capture the culprit himself. The good luck fell to a rookie who had come upon the fellow asleep on the side of the roadway winding around East Rock. He was wearing Mr. Stroebe's suit and Mrs. Casey's squirrel fur-piece was wrapped around his neck. The remainder of the loot was in a big burlap bag which he was using as a pillow. The clock with the window-case works was at his side, the chime set for 8 o'clock.

Later, according to the story in the papers, he was discovered to be a harmless half-wit—half starved. When asked by the police sergeant why he hadn't sold the clock or the silver platter, he said simply, "Only a crook would do that, sir."

Years later, when I wrote home from Camp Jessup, Georgia, that I expected my commission shortly and would need about $150 for a tailor-made uniform, leather puttees, etc., I knew in my heart, when the money order arrived several days later, that most of what it represented, if not all, had come out of accumulations in that little battered old teapot, the funny bowl with the tail-knotted dragons and the little vase with the faded roses.

The Raise

One night, when Pa came home there was an air about him that was peculiar and not easy to define. He looked important and it was apparent that, though he seemed to be frowning, actually he was endeavoring with great difficulty to keep from smiling or even laughing out loud.

My mother noticed it as we sat around the big table in the kitchen, waiting for her to serve the supper. First of all, instead of offering his little wisecracks and delivering his cargo of minor stories picked up during the day—a pleasant habit of his which I have always remembered with an inner glow—he was unusually quiet and reserved. Even when my sister and I babbled about the trivial events of our backyard and school and asked him a few questions, he seemed to be lost in thought, answering only with a vague smile and an absent stare.

Mama was disturbed by this abstraction. Ours was not a household where inhibitions or moods were tolerated or condoned. I recall distinctly that she was stirring something in a pot on the stove, her sweet face flushed from the heat. She turned to Pa and inquired, "What's wrong with you? The tooth again? You're like a baby. A thousand times I've told you—a hundred thousand times—go to the dentist. Have it out."

My father looked up and said calmly, "I got my raise today!"

There must have been other raises before this, but I recall only this particular night and this particular pay boost. Mama stood there at the stove, the mixing spoon poised in one hand. With the other hand, she reached for the end of her apron and wiped her face. Then she said, "You should have gotten it long ago. They waited a long time."

She went back to her chores at the stove and said nothing more, but gradually we were aware she was humming and suddenly she sang out a fragment of the Anna Held song, "I Just Can't Make My Eyes Behave."

Otherwise she seemed unperturbed by the momentous news, but to me and my sister this was awesomely exciting. "The Raise" had been discussed before over the table and on Sunday afternoons and occasionally during those gentle hours just before bedtime. And now it had come! Papa had the raise!

During supper, my father said, "I think Saturday I will go down to Church Street and buy a suit. I think I need a new suit."

My mother said, "Everybody's got a davenport in the front room. Only we haven't got one. All our friends have davenports, but the Sobols have no davenport. Aunt Clara comes from New York. Where can we put her up? If we had a davenport, then comes the night, it opens up like a bed and Aunt Clara sleeps in it nice and comfortable like a lady. Like a queen—and it's no trouble."

Papa cracked his first little joke of the day. He said, "I'll buy my suit, and if Clara comes, I tell you what we do. I'll take the Morris chair and I'll put blankets on it and then I'll put on my new suit and I'll say to Clara, 'Clara, here is where you're going to sleep tonight.' "

We younger ones giggled at my father's involved joke but my mother exclaimed impatiently, "I don't see why we shouldn't have a davenport. All our friends can have one—but no, we can't have a davenport. It's only a dollar a week—and now you've got the raise . . ."

Pa sighed. "All right—all right then. We'll be high-toned too. We'll have the davenport. Maybe you want me to buy an automobubble—all right we'll buy an automobubble and instead of Aunt Clara coming here, we'll put the davenport into the automobubble and take it to Aunt Clara in New York."

By that time we were all laughing and in fine humor. We trooped into the front room and Mama pointed out where the davenport would show to best advantage—right against the west wall, so that if you sat in it, you would be facing the Custer statuette and the enlargement pictures of Grandma and Grandpa in color in the gold frames which flanked a long mirror on the wall. Mama said she was going to start crocheting some cushion covers right away.

On the following night, Pa and Ma went to the store on Congress Avenue, where the beautiful davenport was studied at great length, its virtues and versatility explained by the eager salesman and the deal finally consummated.

And two days later we all boarded the trolley car and rode to Church Street and walked up the faint narrow little business thoroughfare until we came to the men's store where my father occasionally bought a suit. Here again, there were many conferences, intensive study, the business of taking the garments out to the light, questions and answers—and finally the purchase. Mama insisted Papa must buy a tie to match and two pairs of socks. Then we went over to the big department store on Chapel Street and my mother bought two house dresses, but nothing my father would say would persuade her to invest in a street dress.

"When you get another raise," she said, in rebuke, "maybe I'll get a new dress. So long as I've got the davenport, I'm satisfied."

Papa said, "You'll look funny wearing a davenport when we take a walk." But Mama wouldn't budge.

My father was full of high spirits that week. He began discussing the prospects of selling his old bicycle and buying a new one. That was the week, too, he sculpted a splendid head of Lincoln out of putty on a board.

The raise, by the way, was $2.25!

Sunday Walks

After the Sunday breakfast, featured by those never-to-be-forgotten prune turnovers, my mother's specialty, there was the ecstatic recess with the Katzenjammer Kids, Buster Brown, Lady Bountiful, Happy Hooligan, Little Nemo and all that merry and lovable crew of the Funnies.

Then would come the weekly casual query from my father to Mama, "Well, how about a nice little walk? Come, a little walk will do you good."

And Mama would lament, " 'A walk,' he says. 'A nice little walk.' How can I take a walk with all these dishes? And then I have to start with the dinner and then maybe company comes. And you ask me to take a walk. Take the children for a walk—and I'll take the dishes for a walk."

This was the customary Sunday-morning ritual and I do not recall that it ever varied, except on days of rain or snow. My father always extended the invitation; my mother always refused with the same little joke about "taking the dishes for a walk," and always one or two of us younger ones went along with Pa.

"Remember," was Ma's parting admonition. "Be back

15

by one o'clock, no later. If you don't come back by one, I start eating dinner myself—sharp."

My father would grin and project his own little joke. "I make clocks. I don't go by them." This always fetched a little grin from my mother, too. Then our little walking expedition would get under way, but not before Mama ran after us to adjust a button here, straighten a collar there, or pluck a piece of lint from my suit.

She would stand in the doorway, watching us as we took off, holding one corner of her apron to her cheek, a characteristic gesture. A little away from the house, Pa would turn and wave. That was the signal for Mama to wave and go back to her kitchen.

Papa disdained all exercise in favor of walking except for one brief period when he went a bit cuckoo over cycling. It was nothing for him to walk four or five miles a day—just for the lift it gave him, he said. He was a rapid walker and my mother and we children rarely were able to keep up with him, but on Sundays he contented himself with a leisurely pace.

As we strolled along, he sang softly—snatches of melody, fragments of lyrics from current and past songs. Old-timers like "Goodbye, Little Girl, Goodbye," "Just Break the News to Mother" and the snappy, "Where Did You Get That Hat?" Sometimes we tried to join in, but we never managed to carry on because he would grin and we would giggle, and then, when he tried to start all over again, he would stop.

His favorite story concerned his attempt to enlist for the Spanish-American War. He was rejected because he limped. When he explained it was a temporary limp caused by an excessively tight shoe, he was told to return when the limp had disappeared. So a few weeks later, he started back for the recruiting office and was less than a block away when he ran—to avoid an oncoming horse and buggy—and fell, spraining the other foot.

Before he married Mama, Pa was an actor in a New Haven stock company and, I am told, quite an excellent one, excelling in comic parts. But to hear him tell it, he could be quite sad as a tragedian. Then there came an opportunity to go to New York for a part in a play, but Mama, who had just become his wife, put her foot down on that and said she did not want her husband to be an actor because the stage was notoriously immoral, and although she trusted Papa, she did not want him treading the path of temptation. Pa gave up the stage.

Then he thought he would like to be a writer. Now it was Grandma and Grandpa who were upset and urged Mama not to let him embark upon such a foolhardy career. Whenever he told us about this, on these walks, I felt quite despondent. Papa would assure us, despite the protests, he had written stories and articles and had even started a play which he had never finished. He never sold one of his masterpieces, but the pain eased when he became interested in doing water-color paintings and clay and putty sculpture. I still have the Indian head he made out of putty.

But Pa's most beloved art hobby was peculiar. He would collect broken crockery—and, indeed, our friends all saved their shattered dishes and vases for him. With the aid of plaster of Paris, putty and a little gold paint, he would fashion out of these fragments ornate vases or bizarre statuary or weird grotesques.

My mother used to fuss and scold because of the litter he made and complain that, while most women had husbands who were handy around the house, she had a man who was always wasting his time on broken crockery, water colors and the like.

But I remember there never was an occasion when folks came to our house that Ma didn't fetch out Pa's latest creation and boast about it. She would also fib a bit about the cash offers that had been made for it, but which Pa had refused.

Actually, Pa's art was not commercial; at least he never made any money out of it.

But there was another talent which yielded occasional revenue. Having been an actor, Pa was really good at monologues. He had a repertoire of about a half dozen spirited recitations, most of them highly melodramatic. Every so often, he would draw an assignment at a lodge gathering and occasionally even at one of the bigger benefits in a theatre. His favorite was one which detailed the woes of a certain Dr. Brown who had maltreated a few patients. It was a tear jerker—and especially effective on blizzardy or rain-drenched nights. Pa's customary fee was $5 for his one-man show which ran usually for more than an hour. He thought it was the easiest money he had ever earned.

Pa had been a watchmaker's apprentice in early boyhood and because there was rent to pay for our tiny flat and another mouth to feed when I arrived, he decided he would work at his trade. He continued at it until late in 1946, when, over his protests, he was retired on a pension. He thought the new regime of the watch factory was extremely short-sighted in voluntarily surrendering his services and though the blow was softened by a tender, appreciative note from the general manager himself on behalf of all the officials, Pa just couldn't understand it. He was quite a lost soul for a few weeks, unable to enjoy the permanent holiday, but gradually he found comfort in returning to his long-neglected art. He worked occasionally with the putty—more often with the broken pieces of crockery—and in between times helped Ma with the dishes and the housework.

But to get back to those days. Once he soared to the dizzy heights of superintendent of a large watch company in New Jersey, but the duties became distasteful when bad times arrived and he was compelled to dismiss employees. Pa spent many sleepless nights over that—and he told us he wanted never again to be in a position which forced him to discharge people.

If Pa was disappointed because he did not become a great actor or artist or sculptor, he never revealed it. He may have had some high hopes for me. When, one day, I drew a picture of Lincoln which did look something like the President, Pa was certain I would be an artist. Then there was a time he thought I would become a fine musician. I failed him as an artist and as a pianist, but he wasn't reproachful. He would not permit me to learn watchmaking, however, and insisted I must have at least a high school education. I think he was happy that eventually I became a newspaperman because Pa at one time wanted to write for newspapers himself. To his way of thinking, strange to say, there is something literary about newspapermen.

In all honesty, however, I must break down at this point and confess that the footlights, camera and grease paint have beckoned occasionally and I have not been able to resist their enticements. Thus at the age of four, I had a small speaking part in an amateur play which starred my father as comedian. At sixteen I was a supernumerary with William Faversham in *Julius Caesar* and later a "hanger on" with George Arliss in *Disraeli*. I earned $2 a night as a Senator with Faversham and $1.50 with Arliss. In later years, I was even the star who headlined the last big-time Palace vaudeville bill. Subsequently

I headed my own unit in Loew's State, starred in a series of Universal shorts and finally and more recently portrayed myself in a full-length picture, *Copacabana*. Were you to take all the lines I have uttered in the distinguished acting career I have here outlined, string them together, with proper punctuation, I assure you, all told, they would not add up to 100 words!

For several years, Pa made some extra change by taking orders for crayon enlargements. Neighbors dug up old photographs and, within a few weeks, they had a beautiful arty reproduction in colors, very ornately framed. There was an easel in the attic and I often saw Pa daubing away at a rough outline of the subject's features. I took it for granted the drawing was all his. It wasn't until long afterward that I learned it was done by a photographic process and that even most of the shading and coloring was done elsewhere. Then the ensemble was delivered to Pa, who, in turn, delivered it to the customer.

We learned many things about Pa on our walks and also tugged from him his personal philosophy. Thus I recall that one day I inquired about God. Did God have a beard or just a tiny mustache, like my father's? Was He tall or small? What language did He speak? Did He have only two eyes and two ears?

Without a second's hesitation, my father solved the whole puzzle of the Creator. God, he said, was a Wonderful Being who was just the right size, so that no matter how tall a person was, God was just a bit taller and a person had to look up to Him. And His face was so wonderful that if you admired light skin, God's was light and radiant and His hair was blonde and His eyes blue. But if you liked brunettes, then God was black-haired and His eyes were dark brown. He had two ears, but He heard everything even when He slept, and He had two eyes which saw everything even when they were closed.

Above all, my father said, God approved mightily of people who walked a great deal because whoever kept walking stayed out of trouble.

It was simple enough a philosophy, I suppose, but it instilled a great love and admiration for God in us—and a great faith.

Usually we stopped off at a friend's house, where the reward was a piece of candy or a cookie. Then it was a delight to eavesdrop while my father told his repertory of funny stories. We would always laugh, whether we got the point or not.

One story was told so often that I have never forgotten it. It went back many years to a tiny hamlet in a European country. His grandmother had come running into the house, shrieking, "The ducks are dead! The geese are dying!" Papa's grandpa and uncles and aunts ran out into the yard, and sure enough, there were the ducks on their backs, their legs in the air. And there were the geese, almost a hundred of them on their backs, their legs in the air, too.

A few were still flopping about, but before their very eyes, these too, gave up the ghost. The news spread all over the hamlet. Terror froze the villagers. What was this mysterious force which had stricken the fowl?

At sundown several of the uncles piled the bodies into a cart and slowly the oxen plodded down the road with their sad cargo toward the marshes, where they were dumped.

The following morning, my great-grandmama came running into the house shrieking, "The ducks are back! The geese are back! A miracle!"

Out ran great-grandpapa, the uncles and the aunts—and sure enough, there were the ducks, gayly waddling about.

There were the geese in their best strut. Naturally, the hamlet was bewildered, and slightly scared, too. This miracle of miracles—what was the explanation? The ducks and geese had died. The ducks and geese had been resurrected!

That night, a neighbor who had been away for two days returned—and an hour later rushed into the house of my great grandpapa. He was tearful. He was hysterical. His wine had vanished—leaked out during his absence. Gone! His entire season's work. A giant cask had sprung a leak. Into the back yard of my father's grandpa the river of wine had streamed. And so the mystery was cleared. The ducks and the geese had gone on a binge and landed on their backs, stewed to the feathers!

Papa had dozens of stories to tell, vowing always that they were true—that either he, personally, or his folks, or his close friends, had figured actively in them. There was never a dull moment when we went on our Sunday morning walks.

We always managed to be back in the house before my mother's deadline—1 o'clock. The kitchen was a welcome haven, then. The big table would be set. A pitcher of lemonade with either strawberry, grape or raspberry jam, lending color and additional flavor, would furnish the center attraction. Mama would be fussing around the stove, lifting the lid of one pot here, dipping a spoon in to taste the contents of another, opening the oven door to peek in at the chicken or the roast.

After the quick wash-up—at the kitchen sink—we sat down to the Sunday dinner.

"See anybody?" my mother would ask, as she served the soup.

"Teddy Roosevelt," my father would reply. "He wants

me to be an ambassador. I told him no—the watch shop couldn't get along without me."

I wondered how Papa could possibly have seen Teddy Roosevelt while we were along because I knew practically everyone we had encountered on our walk, and Teddy Roosevelt wasn't among them. Also, I was quite impressed by the fact that the great big clock factory couldn't get along without my father. I felt he was a very important fellow, indeed.

Eviction on a Sunny Afternoon

There had been a light drizzle, but sharply at noon, as if the whistle had been blown for it, the sun came out. If you had sufficient imagination, you would wager there was sweet fragrance on this reclaimed street of the Manhattan slums, called Allen. I had no business in the neighborhood, but I was in a hurry to keep an appointment uptown, so I had taken this East Side route from my office on South Street.

Furniture was piled in front of the tenement house, and a woman who might have been thirty or sixty was sitting in a straight-back chair. She sat in the chair stiffly, and all around her were her possessions. There was a birdcage, but no bird was in it. There were two overstuffed chairs and a shabby maroon settee. Pans and pots had been tied together with rope, and there was a bundle of old newspapers with the funnies on top.

The bed frame was perched up in a crazy slant, and on the ground, spread out obscenely, was the raw mattress. A parchment hood for a floor lamp rested on a commode. There were figures of fauns, dancing and blowing on pipes, running all around the hood. A small two-burner gas-range, an old-fashioned icebox, two unopened boxes of soda-crackers, a few empty milk bottles, a phonograph, a toy train with a battered engine, a circular electric heater which gave out a dull glow as it mirrored the sun—all these were among the strewn clutter.

A boy of seven or eight stood near the woman. He did not seem to understand what this was all about. A few neighbors tried to talk to the woman, but she stared at them blankly. Every so often the cop came along and chased curious kids away.

"Get!" he thundered. He said nothing to the woman,

but he didn't seem too happy about having her sitting there with all that furniture around.

A fattish man made notes on a piece of paper as he surveyed the confusion on the sidewalk. He whispered to the woman, but she shook her head. This seemed to annoy him, and he muttered to himself and went back to making more notes on his piece of paper. A big black car slowed down, and from the back seat a woman in a mink coat stared intently. She leaned forward to say something to the driver and the car halted. The woman did not come out of the car, however. She merely stared at the little sidewalk scene. Then she leaned forward again, said something to the man at the wheel and the car pulled away.

One old woman wearing a shaitel, *which was thrust back on her head slightly to reveal a rim of her own gray hair in front, pushed through the cluster of neighbors and went over to the woman in the chair. She spoke in Yiddish.*

"Hust eppis g'essen?" *(Have you had anything to eat?) she asked.*

The woman in the chair shrugged her shoulders, but said nothing.

The neighbor in the shaitel *said in Yiddish, "I'll bring you a nice cup of tea and some cake. You must eat." She went away.*

Now the boy went digging through the pile, and finally he tugged out a large oil-cloth covered picture book. He sat down on the mattress and began looking at the pictures. Some neighborhood kids flocked around. One little girl went over to the boy and studied the pictures, too.

The cop came back and chased the kids. It seemed for a second he wanted to say something to the woman in the chair. He looked at her, but he said nothing. He did order the other women and a few men who had gathered to keep

25

moving. *They didn't budge an inch. Only the cop moved, walking back to the corner.*

The ancient matron in the shaitel *returned. She had a glass of tea which she carried in the saucer, also two pieces of sponge cake, resting on the side of the saucer. She brought no napkin.*

"Na—a bissle varrums," *she said. (Here—something warm). Mechanically the woman in the chair took the cake. She bit into a lump of sugar and then sipped some tea. She did not touch the cake.*

The kids had started a game of catch. The woman in the chair set the glass carefully on the saucer. She turned to the boy, still busy with his picture book.

"Milton," *she screamed,* "why you're sitting there? Go —go play ball with the boys."

Then she went back to her tea.

CHAPTER TWO

Houses in the Raw

Adventure beckoned almost from the moment a group of men straggled into a vacant lot on an early Spring morning. They were unkempt characters of many nationalities and usually they would unpile from huge horse-drawn trucks. From the big wagons, they would unload shovels, pick-axes and more cumbersome implements. We knew what this meant: a new house was going up in the neighborhood.

We extracted every last ounce of fun out of these building activities, fun that endured with exquisite variations until the final nail had been driven in, the ultimate splash of paint applied.

The preliminary excavation became a deep, treacherous valley in which we were isolated thousands of miles from civilization, with Indians or African savages on our trail, ready to do us in.

When the foundation was laid, we fought to the last man from our fortress stronghold, holding the enemy at bay until reinforcements arrived. Sometimes they did not arrive, and we died, one by one, in the most excruciating agony, but with our flag flying bravely, and no whimpering.

27

The siege always ended at 6 o'clock, of course, when we had to go home for supper.

It was when the carpenters arrived and started putting up the first or second floors that the fellows in my neighborhood began to live dangerously. We walked the ribs of the wooden skeleton. We clung from beams and worked our way across to each other. We were pirates now, trying to escape from the foulhearted blackbeard captain or we were making our tortuous way across a bottomless ravine, hand-by-hand over a rope fastened between two mountain peaks. There was hidden treasure on the other side and implacable foes with poisoned arrows.

Once I fell—three stories—to the unfinished cellar below. To this day I carry the scar on my jaw, but it is a badge well worth the pain in which I earned it. That day, the lads permitted me to be leader. Permitted? Insisted, I should say. In absentia—while the druggist was patching up my chin and bandaging my knee.

Far more was involved in the building of a house than the adventure it offered. While the structure was rising, we never were in want for kindling wood. It was an unwritten law that all the scraps were permissible loot for the neighborhood kids. There were short chunks of wood, and strips—and occasionally midget beams. No one in authority frowned or stopped us or chased us when we carried our booty away. Day after day, I used to take home an armload, and ultimately enough to keep the good old kitchen stove supplied for the entire season.

My mother, with her practical sense of humor, would sigh, "Wouldn't it be nice if they built houses out of coal?" And my father would carry on from there and remark, "I know a city where they make houses of chocolate cake and the roof is all ice cream—in three flavors."

I took these observations seriously and for weeks pleaded

with my father to take me to the city where the houses were built of chocolate cake with roofs of ice cream. Also, I began dreaming of homes built of coal, picturing myself carrying away bucketfuls of the left-over coal fragments.

Once, from slabs of discarded lumber, Pa built me a sled with runners fashioned out of the thin steel spokes of an old bicycle wheel. He was quite proud of the finished job, and, looking back now, I realize how keenly hurt he must have been when I protested I didn't want a home-made sled but a bought one—like those the other fellows had. He tried to convince me the one he had constructed was far superior to those new-fangled Flexible Flyers, but he never did sell me on the idea. But a few weeks later, he yielded and let me pick one out at the store.

We often wondered who was to occupy the new house when it was completed. The elders were not above wondering, either, because that became the chief topic of conversation in the grocery store and bakery.

Once a neat two-story house was completed, and an elderly man and a sweet-faced woman who looked young enough to be his daughter moved in. The sweet-faced woman rarely came out in the daytime, but when she did she wore dark glasses such as blind people frequently affect. Average citizens didn't go in for sun glasses as they do nowadays. On these occasions, she was accompanied either by the man (he was her husband, we learned in time) or by an elderly woman who, according to Grocer Schmidtzl, was both companion and housekeeper.

But at night, whenever we ran into the couple, the woman wore no glasses. It was months before my mother discovered that the woman was afflicted with a rare eye affliction which made her almost totally blind in daylight but gave her the acute vision of an owl in darkness.

These new neighbors mingled with none of us—and

the little we were able to unearth about them was conveyed by the storekeepers with whom we all did business.

Then the neighborhood gradually became aware that the husband hadn't been seen with the woman for several weeks. More weeks passed and the woman with the queer eyes was accompanied only by the elderly companion. Once, when I lingered in Lum Lee's laundry around the corner, she came in and I heard her speak for the first time—a soft, husky voice it was. She inquired about some pillow slips Lum Lee was doing up for her.

After she left, Lum Lee yielded to my pleas and handed me a long noodle-like "reefer" which I smoked wickedly. I had the ecstatic feeling I was going to the dogs. As I smoked, I built day dreams about the mysterious woman with the dark glasses. She was Sleeping Beauty besieged by foul vandals and I was going to rescue her and marry her and rule over the kingdom.

The husband never was seen again, but the pretty woman with the owl-eyes lived on in the house with her companion —and was still there when we moved out of the neighborhood to another section. Nor did we ever get to the bottom of the mystery. Once my mother had the brilliant inspiration to inquire of Mr. O'Reilly, the letter carrier, whether the woman received any mail.

Mr. O'Reilly said yes, regularly she received two letters a week postmarked Salt Lake City, and occasionally, a letter or so in different handwriting from other towns. That was all he knew, Mr. O'Reilly insisted.

My mother was disappointed, but I wasn't. I had made the discovery of a city with a fabulous name, and because of an association with the Biblical story of Lot's wife I pictured a far-away place where all the inhabitants were turned into pillars of salt.

My mother wept a little the day my father came home from the shop and announced jubilantly that he had bought The House!

We had never owned a house before, nor, in fact, until this time had we ever occupied a home in complete privacy. Always there had been either an upstairs or a downstairs neighbor.

Now The House was ours—all ours.

For months, the subject had been under discussion. Papa had risen to a minor executive post in the big watch factory. In addition he had earned a few extra dollars, handling a trivial real-estate deal or two, and when one of these transactions had yielded him $150 in cash—a sum which I don't believe he had ever had at one time before— he began to dream about a home of his own.

Then one day he had discovered this gem of a property. On a Sunday afternoon Mama and I dressed up in our best and were taken by trolley car to Dwight Street and then walked eagerly down a block and a half to The House. There was a strange, smallish and baldish man waiting outside. After he had shaken hands with my father and then with my mother, who blushed shyly when he told her what a good-looking woman she was, we entered.

The House was two and a half stories high. It boasted a huge kitchen, a dining room and a front room on the first floor, and three bedrooms and a bathroom on the second. Below there was a cellar with a large furnace, and above there was an attic. The sight of that attic was all I needed to start planning The Club I would organize and be president of, with members at my beck and call to read the nickel thriller novels, play miggles and produce the stirring dramas I was sure I could improvise.

There was a fine boiler in the kitchen connected with the stove and the smallish man explained enthusiastically: "Hot water all day long—no fuss, no bother. There it is— hot water while that stove keeps burning." This seemed much too wonderful and unbelievable, for there had been no boiler in the other places we had called home. Hot water for the Saturday bath had been boiled in big pots on the kitchen stove. Now we had a boiler, and that meant hot water for washing hands on cold mornings. I now realize what happy thoughts rippled through my mother's mind at the prospect of hot water whenever she wanted it for washing dishes and clothes.

So we moved into the beautiful house. Though from time to time there was some vague and mysterious and what must have been worried talk about the mortgages, I went on blissfully ignorant of these tedious details. Owning a house, as my father did, meant we were rich, for there was no rent to pay.

A month after we moved in, Spring came in too. My mother began planting flower seeds, while my father busied himself after work in the spacious backyard where he was going to raise tomatoes, celery, radishes and other greens.

For several nights, too, there was a discussion about chickens. My father who was handy with carpenter tools (and also liked to trim my hair and repair our shoes) started to build a coop. Mama tried to persuade him that she would have very little time to take care of the chickens. Besides, their cackling annoyed her, she said.

Pa went ahead with the coop just the same. When it was completed, he used it to store the lawnmower and the carpenter tools. I used it whenever I wanted to play bandits with the gang.

The flowers came up beautifully and the vegetables in the backyard responded enthusiastically to my father's gentle care. Each evening when Pa came home from work, just before we settled down for supper, he and Ma would walk out to the front yard, so that she could indicate the new flowers which had blossomed. Then they would walk round to the backyard and Pa would study his vegetables, flick at a potato bug, pick up a stone or pluck a weed.

One morning when my mother was out of the house, I heeded the suggestion of an older buddy who lived two doors away to pluck out the radishes and other vegetables. We piled them into a basket and off we went on a sales jaunt. The neighborhood selected was three blocks away and susceptible territory, for we disposed of our loot in short time. I split twenty-five cents with my confederate. That is, I gave him ten cents and kept fifteen. He didn't demur at this arrangement, when I pointed out that after all it had been my backyard which had been the source of our supplies.

That night when my father came home and went out to the garden as usual, I began to experience some doubt as to the wisdom of my business enterprise. In fact, I was convinced a few minutes later that perhaps it had been a grave error. Pa came storming into the house and demanded to know who had been in the garden and pulled up all the vegetables.

Young George Washington is reputed to have confessed he chopped down that historic cherry tree. The Spartan boy let the fox gnaw at his breast without whimpering. I had half a dozen sterling examples out of the Second and Third Readers. I ignored them. I did not confess.

I pretended not to hear even. My father turned to me and kept inquiring, each time a bit angrier than before, whether I knew anything about the marauders. I remained silent.

So too will I remain completely mute about what happened immediately thereafter. I have never cared much for vegetable gardens since that day.

Now that we had The House, Pa became a prodigious laborer in pursuit of his artistic hobbies. In the cellar, in addition to his workshop, he had a studio as well. Here he worked with his broken crockery, creating his vases and unique frames and statuary. For variation, he shifted over to his putty, sculpting heads of notables. He must have fashioned at least three George Washingtons, four Abraham Lincolns, and any number of Indian Chiefs during these years. In another corner of the cellar stood his easel. When he tired of his other plastic undertakings, he would brush away in oils or draw a little scene in crayon. In winter the only interruption he would allow himself was getting up to pay a little personal attention to the furnace, his special pride and joy.

Against my mother's protests, Pa decided he would build the screen doors himself. He started in the Spring, working in his spare time after shop hours and on Sundays. Late in June, when the hot days began crowding in on us, he had them completed.

There were no special ceremonies planned for the Big Day—the day when the doors were to be fitted on to their summer hinges—but Pa went around humming and there was an attitude of I-am-the-Conqueror about him. An uncle had remained overnight, and he and Pa went down into the cellar to bring up the doors.

The moment was tense as Pa and Uncle started to attach those doors. My mother stood there, a trifle nervous, holding a corner of her apron to her mouth in her characteristic gesture when some emotion was disturbing her, and we younger ones, our ranks augmented by a few of our eager and curious playmates, crowded around. Contrary to my mother's fears and in rebuttal to my uncle's good-natured jibes, those screen doors over which Pa had labored for many weeks in the cellar fitted perfectly!

The job done, Pa slapped my uncle jubilantly on the back, looked over at Ma triumphantly and shouted, "See! A machine couldn't make it better."

Then with a sly look at Ma, he suggested, "Would you like me to make you new window shades?"

My mother shuddered at the very idea and earnestly pleaded with him not to try to make anything else for the house. To my uncle she explained, apologetically, "When he goes into that cellar he forgets he has a wife, a home, children. He forgets he has to eat. He forgets everything. It's cheaper to buy the things."

But Mama's protests couldn't spoil Pa's day of triumph. For weeks thereafter, whenever we had company, he would show them those screen doors, explain in detail how he had worked out the exact measurements, how he had tacked in the screening, his special tactics with the hinges, handles and snap lock.

In time, those fine home-made screen doors under the assaults of summer storms and impatient youthful knees and hands began to develop signs of dropsy, swelling of the joints and mumps. The wooden frames became warped and the screening bulged out. We never seemed to have time to open the doors gently, turning the handle first, but usually prodded the screening with our knees or hands and occasionally with a shoulder.

One of us discovered that if you worked your pencil through the screen it would spread the little hole. Not a particularly novel or momentous discovery, I confess, but one which gave me the kind of pleasure boys get only out of destruction. Making big holes out of little holes had less appeal for Pa. When he caught me at it one day, I lost all interest in the pastime.

As I recall The House, it was large and beautiful with spacious grounds and an inviting front porch. There seemed room for everything and everyone. Not so many years ago, haunted with a hunger to see again the only home we had ever owned, I returned to Dwight Street. The House had shrunk. It seemed pitifully small from the outside. All of it, house and grounds, appeared to be as shabby as the old man who was then sitting on the front porch, smoking his pipe.

Now I wish I had never gone back to see The House.

The First Piano

When I first became aware that my father and mother were serious about buying a piano, my impulse was to shout to the world: "We're going to have a piano. Hooray, we're going to have a piano."

There was no telephone in our house—very few people in our neighborhood had telephones at this period. Otherwise the Coming Event would have been announced far and wide.

But most of our neighbors did have pianos, and it had been a point of extreme humiliation to me that only our household was barren in this respect. My mother, and occasionally my father, in answer to inquiries, told me gently that pianos cost a great deal of money, and we had none to spare. Frankly, I was quite vague about the necessity of a piano, since none of us knew how to play. Somehow an upright or a grand seemed an essential piece of furniture in a Connecticut home. It was a symbol of gentility and security.

So there came the day when I knew eventually we, too, were to be blessed with a piano. There were many difficulties to overcome, of course. First we had to accompany the furniture man to a wholesaler who had an entire floor cluttered up with pianos of all sizes and prices.

Each of these had to be studied carefully, not for quality of tone—none of us knew a thing about that—but for color, size, price, etc.

My mother thought a baby grand would fit into our living room and take up space now occupied by some ancient pieces she wanted to donate to a second cousin. My father was dead set against this choice for a sound reason: the price was prohibitive. My mother pointed out, with her customary feminine logic, price didn't make much difference; the down-deposit would be only a matter of a few extra dollars which she volunteered to contribute out of one of her teapot banks, and then it would be only a matter of another fifty cents a week on the installments. Pa said it was too great an undertaking and finally—this was a rare occasion, believe me—he prevailed, and we settled upon a fine upright in a dark mahogany finish. I think the trade name was "Llewellyn." At any rate, I seem to recall it was crowded with l's.

The furniture man patted me on the head and said, "Sit on the stool, sonny. Go on, sit on the stool. Take a ride."

I settled myself on the piano stool and the furniture man gave me a gentle push. I went around and around. It made me very dizzy.

There was some disappointment connected with the momentous transaction. First, there were imposing papers to be filled out—some names to be signed which I know now were to be a guarantee that my father would faithfully keep up his payments of $2 a week until the piano was fully paid for. Then, too, we must expect there would be a delay of perhaps two or three weeks, as the piano was to be shipped from the factory.

However, the interim gave me an opportunity to let the neighborhood know I had a great secret. I merely let the hints fall here and there that a bit of urging might tug the secret from me. We were going to have a piano in our house. A magnificent hunk of furniture! By the time I was through describing the rare instrument, adding some fantastic embellishments, the girls and boys and the adults, too, I think, were convinced it was being imported from some distant land like Turkey or Egypt and it was the only one of its species in all the world.

The great day arrived. A truck pulled by two huge percherons drew up to our front door and a massive wooden crate was unloaded. Right on the sidewalk, the boards were ripped off—and there she was, this dream of a piano, shiny and new in all its glory there against our front lawn.

There were consultations and advice offered by my father and the neighbors to the truckmen, instructing them just how to get it through the front door into the parlor. The movers said, No—not through the doorway—but through the window. My father scoffed at the idea. Then he learned something—and so did I. The men calmly removed the windows, and now with wide straps and pulleys, with heaving and tugging, the piano was pulled through. Then my mother and several of the neighbors went into a serious huddle to decide where it should be placed for the best effect.

My father passed a pitcher of beer over to the movers and politely joined them for a glass of cheer. Some of the men neighbors joined in. One of the truckmen, expanding, described a horrendous experience when a grand piano, while being lifted to the third story of a house not many blocks away, had slipped from its halter and crashed to the ground. He was very gloomy as he recalled the incident.

When everything was settled and my mother had polished the piano from top to bottom, scrubbed the keys, gently flicked the strings inside with a flimsy cloth, she took off her apron, patted her lovely brown hair, looked coyly over at my father and then at me—and proceeded to sit down and let her fingers roam over the keys. Of course she couldn't read a note. But she pushed the keys down—and giggled over the discords. She let her hand ripple the full length of the keyboard. It sounded wonderful and we told her so. My father said, "Why don't you take lessons when Louie does?"

Then it was I knew for the first time I was to learn how to play the piano. It had never occurred to me. My day dreams began at once. I would be a great musician and everyone would invite me to parties and I would play songs while everyone exclaimed, with awe and even envy, "Isn't he wonderful? The way he plays—it's wonderful! How did he learn to play? He's so young!" No, said my mother. A mother with three children—how could she take piano lessons? It was silly. Louie would learn how to play and then, when he knew how—maybe he would teach her.

Now there were conferences with the neighbors again. There was a choice between a certain Miss Eckstein, an inoffensive, good-natured young woman and quite pretty, whose fees were reasonable—thirty-five cents for an hour's lesson—and Lucy Pinelli, a moody elderly spinster of Italian parentage who, it was whispered, had studied in Rome! Miss Pinelli's fee was fifty cents for only half an hour!

There was a week of debate. Should the pianistic career

of the future DePachmann be entrusted to the amiable, rather frivolous Miss Eckstein who, like as not, might even bring one of her several young suitors along with her to wait patiently while she instructed her young charge? Or should the task fall to the happy lot of the unprepossessing Miss Pinelli?

Miss Pinelli seemed to care less about men than music. She taught the two daughters of old Schwarz, who ran the blacksmith shop; the younger McCarthy boy whose father owned a drugstore; the niece of our school principal and the sister of the bachelor head of the Dime Savings Bank.

Miss Pinelli won out. I was to start with half-hour lessons on Friday afternoons after school. Later, my mother assured Miss Pinelli, if I made proper progress and revealed sufficient enthusiasm, perhaps the period would be extended to an hour.

"If he does not show progress," said Miss Pinelli, coldly, "I will not come here. There must be the spark— willingness, love for music. If he has it, good—good. If not, you must get someone else."

I found myself disliking her intensely.

Frankly, at the beginning I was more fascinated with the little machine, which, at the behest of Miss Pinelli, we bought to be placed on top of the piano. It was a contraption with a pendulum attachment which, when set off, swung from side to side, making a click-click noise. Many years later I learned the little machine was called a metronome. Although Miss Pinelli insisted it was essential to develop the proper sense of rhythm, I never did get the hang of the little doohickey in relation to the pieces I played on the piano.

As the months marched by and I progressed from scales to simple little melodies, to a point even where I crossed my hands occasionally and was beginning to be called upon to play for company, I never overcame my dislike of the tall, sharp-eyed, sharp-tongued old maid who was guiding my musical education. There was a harshness about her, an utter lack of warmth, a moodiness that to me lacked the redeeming grace of mystery.

On several occasions I pleaded with my parents to change over to the gentler, gayer, less expensive Miss Eckstein, but my mother said no. Some day I would be grateful I had studied with Lucy Pinelli. She was a great musician and a fine woman, my mother said.

So two years passed and then one afternoon Miss Pinelli failed to make her appearance. We had no telephone—and for that matter neither did the music teacher —so there was no immediate way of learning what had happened.

Very little was known about the woman's private life. She was older than my parents and, personally, I always thought her on the homely side. But listening in on the talk among the older folks, I gathered she had been quite sought after when she was younger and my father said a certain foreman—a widower in his shop—still paid occasional court to her.

It was not until late that night that the mystery of Miss Pinelli's non-appearance was cleared. Mr. Cutler, the milkman, arriving at her tiny three-room flat for his weekly collections had knocked at the door repeatedly, and, finally, finding it unlocked, had walked in. On the floor of the kitchen in front of the small range, he saw the sprawled body of the music teacher. She was dead.

On the range, a soup had boiled over, splotching the pot and the top of the stove. Through the doorway of the kitchen looking into a small bedroom, Mr. Cutler saw a young man in bed and by the side of the bed a wheelchair. A hopelessly paralyzed, speechless young man whom he and the landlord and perhaps one or two others knew to be the husband of the sharp-faced, thinnish, unlovely old woman.

This was Miss Pinelli's great secret that we younger ones knew nothing about, and, for that matter, few of the elders knew either. Evidently she had been preparing the noon-day dinner for him when her heart gave out, and the end came.

The gay Miss Eckstein began coming to our house the following Friday.

My mother never did find time to take lessons. After a few years daily practice became irksome to me, especially when Spring rolled around. I gave up taking lessons, and my sister began.

The piano remained with the folks for many years and then it passed to a younger sister who sold it one day for junk and bought herself a new and up-to-the-minute affair. She rarely uses it. For her radio and recorded music is much sweeter.

Music on a Restless Night

I wandered over to Bill Hardy's place. Bill is my friend. I like him. Once he went dancing around town with a fellow named George Raft, dancing for dimes and quarters. Once he was a riding master. Now, with his pal, Henry Tannen, he operates a colorful joint known as the Gay Nineties—so colorful, so full of oldtime mementoes that I have been advocating that the city step in and take the place over as a Museum of Nostalgia.

I wanted to shut out the war, politics, small chatter and boredom. This was the set-up I needed for my mood—a saloon with the oldtime atmosphere and with a piano always in action. A fellow prodded by a few ancient relics, the proper oldtime tunes, and a working imagination may turn the clock back and have himself a time with his fancies and his memories.

The slim, balding fellow in the loud checked suit with the pinch-back jacket and the brown derby atilt over his rusty dome was pounding out "My Nellie's Blue Eyes" and a fattish gent with a sweet-looking elderly woman at his side tapped his beer glass with a spoon in rhythmic accompaniment. The piano player switched to "Dear Old Girl." "Dear old girl, the robin sings above you. . . . Dear old girl, it speaks of how I love you. . . ."

There were framed theatre programs above me on the wall. Blanche Bates in The Darling of the Gods, young, striking-looking Blanche Bates, and in fine print it was revealed that among the cast was a minor supporting character named George Arliss, playing the role of Zakkuri. Blanche Bates made me think of Blanche Ring. "I got rings on my fingers, bells on my toes. . . ."

There were other programs, yellowed but neat in their

frames. Richard Mansfield in Beaucaire, *Maxine Elliott in Clyde Fitch's* Her Own Way, *David Warfield in* The Music Master—*in the cast a promising young girl named Jane Cowl and an excellent up-and-coming actor named Taylor Holmes.*

The quartet was blending voices harmoniously. "My little girl, you know I love you. . . . And I long for you each day . . ." I wandered over to the row on row of shaving mugs with the names of their owners enscrolled with flourishes in gold. There was that barber shop around the corner from where we lived—and a vague memory of a hope that some day I would have enough hair on my face to entitle me to a fancy shaving mug stuck up in its proper place on the barber's shelf.

"If I had my way, dear, forever there'd be . . . A garden of roses for you and for me." The fat gentleman was joining the quartet, singing to the sweet elderly woman at his side. Wasn't it only a short time ago that I sat here and listened and watched as Al Smith sang in quavering but determined and hoarse voice along with this very same quartet? "Daisy, daisy, give me your answer, do . . ."

I drifted up a flight of stairs to the rococo barroom, right out of the mauve decade. Huge paintings of hefty nudes that once hung in saloons of cherished memories. Big shiny cuspidors—one from the home of the late Chauncey Depew. A faded photo of the Jim Corbett-John L. Sullivan fight and the crowd. An ancient music box, something like those you see in the Bowery penny arcades even today.

This one, after we dropped in a coin, squeaked out, "They called her frivolous Sal—a peculiar sort of a gal." I picked up a few dusty paper-backs—dime novels with lurid, exciting covers. The Doom of Chinatown Nell, Back to Her Sewer, The Gunner-Man.

I went downstairs again. The man at the piano was back. He was singing as he played. "There are smiles—that make

44

us happy . . . Smiles that make us blue." The place was filling up and the room buzzed and hummed with chatter. The fattish gent and the sweet-faced elderly lady were still there. He had fastened a cardboard black mustache under his nose. He looked comical. The sweet-faced lady beamed tenderly.

Reluctantly I left. You can't stay with the past too long.

CHAPTER THREE

Money Is Nice

The weekly wage of the household heads in our neighborhood ranged from $16 to as high as $25. Taxes, of course, were something that affected in a vague way people of immense wealth. I can't recall anyone in our circle ever having to pay taxes.

Most of the men in our neighborhood meekly handed over the weekly pay envelope to their wives and received a daily allowance, rarely in excess of twenty-five cents, because it was the custom to go home for the noon-day meal. Some citizens whose work carried them too far away did take their lunches with them, but no one ever went to the extravagance of eating at a lunchroom during the noon hour.

There was always considerable elation when, four or five times a year, orders at the factory were so heavy that it was imperative to go into overtime. No one received time and a half in those days, but overtime meant more money in the pay envelope and occasionally—very rarely, of course—the management would come through generously with a fragmentary bonus.

Sometimes the overtime swelled the envelope by as

much as $3 or $4, and it was on occasions like these that a fellow's pa would buy him a pair of new shoes or his mother would get that new dress, regretting over and over again out loud because she had squandered $7 on such impulsive foolishness.

It's too bad I can't remember the price of commodities in those days, but I do know it was considered sinful and wasteful and extravagant to buy canned goods—except sardines and salmon. My mother bought fresh vegetables and fruits. When grapes were in season, there was that pleasant period when heavenly aromas drifted from the kitchen when she was making grape jelly. In the cellar or high up in the closets there would be preserved pears and peaches and cherry jam, pickled watermelons and apples— all jarred at home.

I'll never forget my mother's astonishment when, years later, a neighbor said she never bothered to cook soup; she got it out of cans. Until then my mother actually never suspected that even soups came in cans in this advanced era.

Out of the average weekly pay, in addition to her husband's allowance, pennies for the children, money for the rent, kerosene, gas meter, coal, milkman, butcher, etc., the housewife managed to have meat at least four days a week—twice a day. Usually the big meal was at noon. There was always meat left over for supper and then, as now, Friday was the big fish day, and Sunday, the day for roast chicken or stuffed goose. A special delicacy in our home was stuffed chicken's neck, the stuffing consisting of some heavenly mixture of flour, potatoes, etc., over which the thinnish skin of the chicken's neck would be sewed in the form of a sausage.

There was a nice family named Donovan who lived three doors away from us. Mr. Donovan enjoyed something of an advantage over the other men in our neighborhood. He was a street-car conductor, and, four nights a week, he helped out in a saloon over on State Street. We never knew quite how much Mr. Donovan earned as a conductor, but whatever it was, it went to his wife.

But for those four nights in the saloon, where he helped out behind the bar and did other odd jobs, Mr. Donovan received $9. Of this, $6 was set aside for a special fund because Mr. Donovan was going to study law some day, and the remaining $3 was his to do with as he pleased. Naturally, the other men in the neighborhood were quite envious.

One night Mr. Donovan, reaching over the bar to talk to a friend, stuck a finger on a pen which his friend was carrying in the upper pocket of his vest, point up. Five days later, Mr. Donovan was dead from blood poisoning, and Mrs. Donovan discovered among his effects a bankbook disclosing an account which she never knew he had. It revealed that out of the $3 allowance, and occasional tips, he had saved more than $300 in less than three years.

"He was such a thoughtful, saving man," wept Mrs. Donovan.

Every household had its improvised bank—often made of one of those large tins, which looked like miniature trunks—in which the tea came. This would be soldered securely and a slit cut into the top to receive bills and coins. We had one of these—in addition to my mother's little teapot and vase caches—and it was always a great treat for the children to gather around when Pa was going to pry the can open and count the hoard.

Then came the greater thrill of accompanying him to the bank to watch the teller count the coins and the bills and make little notations in the bankbook.

The teller always took time off to chat pleasantly with

Pa about the weather and about that stout man named Taft who was going to run for President. This particular teller never liked Mr. Theodore Roosevelt or his policies and freely admitted it, but my father thought Teddy was wonderful and always reminded the teller that the reason he hadn't been a soldier in the Spanish-American War was because of a temporary limp. If he had been accepted, he undoubtedly would have been a Rough Rider. I think Pa was quite convinced he would have crashed through into Teddy's select group.

Once President Roosevelt rode through our town in an open barouche and my father pushed and elbowed his way and mine through the crowds until we stood where we could see him as clear as day. Then my father waved a hand and yelled, "Hi, Teddy!" and I could swear Teddy's broad beam was directed at just us two—although it occurs to me now, as I think back, it is possible he did not hear my father's salute because at the time the thousands who were lining the walks were roaring, "Hi, Teddy!" too.

Picnics and Holidays

If there were organized camps for us younger ones in those days, certainly none from our neighborhood went to them. Of course, there were some folks who went off to farms or sea resorts for the Summer, but for the most part, they came from the more exclusive neighborhoods. My set was satisfied to run up to the pond in the mornings or in the late afternoons or hike out to the woods. Our fathers rarely had vacations if they worked in the shop or took one if they owned stores. Our mothers got no rest, even on Sundays.

Especially on Sundays!

But we had our picnics. Sometimes just a group of the neighbors made up their own outing. Sometimes it was one church or the other and sometimes a lodge.

It was a tolerant era and the Catholic and Jewish girls and boys went off gaily to outings sponsored by the Protestant Church—or vice versa. Usually, we went by open trolley, occasionally in wagons. The mothers made up sandwiches and cold cuts; the men chipped in for a keg or two of beer. When we reached the picnic grounds, some of the women would get busy making lemonade.

The games were simple. Baseball, foot-races, tug o'war, weight lifting, stone hurling, horseshoe pitching, trick diving and tree climbing. The older boys and girls did a bit of spooning, which met with very little sympathy and much jeering from the hard-boiled younger ones.

Often old Alex Bronson would come along, and then there really would be fun. Bronson who must have been 60 or so at the time, once had been with Lew Dockstader's Minstrels and later played in vaudeville. He had suffered a rare accident in a Chicago theatre. There was a trio of acrobats with whom he used to pal. One night he was waiting in the wings to go on after they had completed their last stunt. Part of the routine called for one of the men to make a triple somersault from the shoulders of one partner to the shoulders of another. Somehow, he came down with such force on the latter that the two fell into the wings on top of Bronson. The acrobats escaped unharmed, but Bronson's back was broken.

He had never worked since. Though he hadn't collected any damages, since he wouldn't sue friends and the theatre disclaimed all responsibility, he had been drawing a small weekly sum from an insurance policy and he was quite content because his back had mended after a fashion and he was able to get about.

At any rate, old Bronson would come out to our picnics and usually he was the life of the party. He told gags. He arranged little skits in which young and old participated. He impersonated famous stars of the day. He did card tricks. Every time old Bronson came to the picnic, he was the talk of the neighborhood for days.

Death came to the old performer one afternoon—and it was a violent death. The flagpole on the Danforth Street school, blown loose from its socket by a strong wind, fell upon Bronson, cracking his skull. He was dead when they picked him up.

One of the reporters, I recall, wrote a story about the old fellow's passing, pointing dramatically to the fact that when the first men reached him after the accident, they found the American flag covering his fine face as if in solemn tribute. Later we learned that this wasn't quite true because the flag had not been flying that day. The truth was less than dramatic. The flagpole had been a roosting perch for many birds. The covering over poor Bronson's face was definitely not a flag of red, white and blue.

My father was never a joiner, but so many of his friends belonged to fraternal organizations that he was always invited to the picnics given by the Moose or the Pythians or the Turn Verein. The Turn Verein outings were the best. The members were Germans who went in for choral singing and for athletics. If they felt any race superiority, certainly they kept it well hidden.

They were a kindly, hospitable group—and to repeat, their picnics were wonderful. It wasn't only because of the food—or the exhibition of calisthenic feats—but the inspiring blending of from 100 to 200 voices in those magnificent German songs. There was something about this great chorus that made young men and young women look at each other dreamy-eyed and hold hands and even wander away a bit into the thicker woods where they could be alone, but not out of hearing of the wonderful voice harmonies.

So Summers passed pleasantly enough, even if we young ones never got off to a camp or a seashore. There was one eventful year, though, when my father earned a little extra money by selling some crayon enlargements of some men who worked in the shop with him. He decided my overworked mother was entitled to a luxurious holiday in the country.

So we went—my mother, my sister, my brother, then a baby, and I—to a wonderful farm outside of East Lyme, Conn., and there we remained from late in March to September. This was the happy period when I spent three months in a country school, where all grades were assembled in one room and taught by the one teacher, a period at a time.

Here I learned about catching buckeyes (a fish a little larger than a herring) with bare hands as they tried to flap back over wooden dams; how to skin a woodchuck; how to pick wild strawberries without contracting ivy-poisoning (the best strawberries were always in the poison-ivy stretches); how to put sugar on a bee-sting wound; how to drink pigeons' eggs raw.

There were a thousand and one delights in this first lengthy stay at a farm, but the greatest I think was the discovery I made upon the very first day we arrived. Embarking upon a tour of exploration before supper, I climbed up into the attic of the ancient farm house and stumbled over the most wonderful treasure trove!

There before me, stacked in neat piles all over the place, were nickel and dime novels dating back five or six years.

Nick Carters, Liberty Boys, Merriwells, Pirate Days, Young Wild West—all of them.

Mine—all mine—to read and reread at leisure. What a glorious season that turned out to be!

Not many years ago I revisited that farm in East Lyme, Conn. The little white schoolhouse was still there, and so was the pond where we used to fish for buckeyes. Later in the moonlight, on the plank-board bridge, I looked down into the dark, softly murmuring pool and drank in the quiet and peace of the frosty, full-mooned night in rural Connecticut, trying to recapture the thrill of those other years.

In vain! For the little white schoolhouse was now a roadside joint. And the calm of that precious night was shortly shattered by a juke-box blast of raucous tunes, reminding me that I had to drive back to New York and my saloon beat!

Collector's Item

Of course, we all had our hobbies, from prized aggies to rare stamps. In fact, most of the fellows in my set were ardent stamp collectors. In those early days, the hobby was simplified for us.

You saved the covers of the shoe-polish cans (Shinola) and for every dozen, the generous company rewarded you with from 50 to 100 of the nicest-looking stamps in all colors of the rainbow—and with the oddest faces.

Unfortunately, my interests were diverted to cigar bands, and Saturday mornings were spent walking along the streets, carefully probing the gutters for the butts with the bands still intact, for those were the days when it was considered very high-toned, indeed, to leave the bands on while smoking.

My father is much to blame for this rather futile hobby because he used to take those bands and create designs with them on plates and pitchers and around ordinary drinking glasses. I think it is only because I was too lazy to plunge into the more exciting and more strenuous pursuit of capturing butterflies that he did not turn to making those bizarre designs with butterfly wings.

Come to think of it, even if I hadn't been so lazy, I should not have gone after butterflies because just about that time I began wearing a handsome little button proclaiming my membership in the S.P.C.A. For weeks, I remember watching carefully at street corners, in the faint hope that perhaps I might detect some driver beating his horse, in which event I was prepared to go up to him and peremptorily command him to stop, by virtue of the authority invested in me by that button.

Do you want to know the truth? Never, through the many months during which I sported that badge, did I encounter a single instance of cruelty to animals.

It was most disheartening.

The Blacksmith Shop

Down the block was the blacksmith shop operated by the brothers Schwarz. We all envied the brothers Schwarz and the happy fate that was theirs—to be able to spend so many days and nights in that wondrous establishment. We would linger around, listening to the delightfully flat melody produced by the clang of the huge hammer against the white-hot horseshoe on the anvil and the softer, sweeter rap against the shoe when it was being nailed to the hoof.

And we envied the Brothers Schwarz for their indifference to soot and smudge and stain of ash, to the heat of the flame spurred by the bellows' prodding breeze—to their indifference, in fact, to everything we had been taught we must not be indifferent to.

A fellow managed to find his way into the blacksmith shop quite accidentally before noon and there was always a generous slice of home-made apple pie, sprinkled with cinnamon and sugar, dripping rich in the juices of the choice apples which formed its body. It was at the blacksmith shop I learned to drink coffee, for the Brothers Schwarz saw nothing criminal in serving the brown pick-me-up to growing youth.

There was admiration for the Brothers Schwarz for the reckless manner in which they handled most of their charges. A horse might kick and prance and stomp and snort and roll wild eyes, but he could not scare the Brothers Schwarz. Off would come the bent or broken or wornout shoe, and on would go the new one. Before the operation was complete, the Brothers Schwarz and Dobbin were on the friendliest of terms.

There were chickens in back of the blacksmith shop, and when we tired of playing in the sand piles in front of the corset factory, we would visit the Brothers Schwarz estate and feed the hens or the rabbits or climb the big maple tree and look into the little birds' house which was usually empty.

Once one of the chickens lay as if dead and both brothers took turns trying to revive it, but it merely fluttered its eyes once or twice and then was limp. One of my buddies, Albert, whose father operated a beer saloon on the corner said he thought his Pop could do something about this, and, though the Brothers Schwarz shook their heads and said no, the chicken was a goner, Albert ran for his Pop nevertheless.

Back came Pop Schlechter, a thinnish, pipe-smoking German. He took his time and advanced with great dignity, wiping his hands on his big white apron. Pop Schlechter studied the limp bird for a few seconds, then picked it up and studied it more intently. He asked for some bread. One of the brothers Schwarz ran into the blacksmith shop and returned with half a loaf.

Pop Schlechter plucked away a tiny mound of the bread, rolled it between his palms, pressed it with his thumb and then stuffed it down the chicken's gullet. He pushed something else down. Whether it was corn or more bread, I don't recall.

But the bird began to show life. Slowly it struggled to its feet, flapped its wings, feebly at first—then, vigorously —and whisht, it went scurrying off, as good and alive as new!

Pop Schlechter wiped his hands again on his white apron and grunted something to Albert about coming along with him, the Brothers Schwarz went back into the blacksmith shop, and I followed them in. A few minutes later Albert came back with a big can of beer and the Brothers Schwarz took turns gulping heartily from the can, but they didn't offer either Albert or me any.

Poverty and Affluence

Two houses down the street, lived the Scarnaskis. The Scarnaskis were the poorest folk in our neighborhood. Every so often, my mother would send over discarded garments and Mrs. Scarnaski would make them over for her brood. Also Mama never made jam or preserves without sending me over with a jar or two for our poverty-stricken neighbors.

Yet the truth is there was no pity in my heart—only scorn—when I first became aware that the Scarnaskis had to depend upon smelly kerosene lamps for their illumination and still had to hie to the primitive little shed in their backyard instead of enjoying the fine modern plumbing that we boasted in our house.

I must have had an impulse for cruelty which prodded me into inviting young Peter Scarnaski over when my father first installed the new-fangled gas-mantle. It was a wondrous contraption that fitted like a gauze glove-finger over the jet and in turn was protected by a frosted glass globe. My father explained that not only were we going to enjoy better light, but actually there was a great deal of economy involved. Peter watched in awe while my father pulled the little chains that came with the marvelous device and graduated the light.

I was determined Peter must be impressed further. So we followed my father down into the cellar, and for the first time my young neighbor had the rare privilege of watching the gas-meter fed with a quarter. Nonchalantly I explained it was nothing in our household to put as many as four to six quarters into that big box daily. Peter, wide-eyed, said nothing, and I was regretful I had been so niggardly in my conservative estimate. I could have said 100 quarters and Peter would have believed me.

However, I had scored. Henceforth nothing would convince Peter Scarnaski whose father earned $11 a week as a night watchman that I was anything but the heir of an extremely wealthy family and that I dwelt amid enviable opulence.

So it was I won for myself a following of one loyal disciple and my ego swelled until it was deflated abruptly one afternoon when I attended a party at a classmate's home on Orange Street. His name was Charles Erbe and his father owned a big drug store. It was no secret to most of us that Charlie was very rich, although he took his state of affluence with becoming modesty, and, in fact, no one had to ask twice to borrow his coaster-brake bike or his genuine pigskin college football (not one of those round, black rubber affairs which most of us possessed).

I went to this party at Charlie Erbe's, and my heart sank. For here was the house of dreams. First of all, at Erbe's there were real electric lights, just like those which were installed in our school. Secondly, the bathroom was right next to the bedroom, and the beautiful and large tile bath-tub had a single shiny faucet so that by regulating the little wheel-knob marked "hot" and the one marked "cold," just the desired degree of warm water was yours, and no trouble at all. Charlie had each of us turn on the water, so we could judge for ourselves how simple it all was.

And then, for the final triumph, he pointed upward, and there most of us beheld for the first time a shower gadget. Charlie wanted to undress there and then, and invited us to do likewise and share this great luxury, but his mother yelled for him to come out of the bathroom. So it was quite a few years later before I had the opportunity of testing for myself and determining what comfort there could be in a shower right in your own bathroom.

But the wonders of this house were not over. Later in the afternoon, when we were in the kitchen, I asked Charlie casually whether he, too, had to empty the icebox basin every day, one of my burdensome chores.

"Icebox basin?" jeered Charlie. "Shucks, we ain't got none. Look!" And then my heart really crumpled in envy. For the Erbe icebox was equipped with a funnel which emptied into a connecting pipe, eliminating the need for the basin to catch the drippings from the melting ice. I made up my mind my folks would know all about this as soon as I could hurry home.

My mother and father listened patiently enough as I recited the wonders of the Erbe home. Finally my father said, "Well, if I owned a drug store . . ." And my mother said, "Everything always looks better in someone else's place."

I screamed, "But, Mom, it is better. Electric lights and a shower thing and no ice pan! It is better."

All that night I felt sorry for myself and the fate that had made me a member of a family which could not afford electricity or shower baths or connected iceboxes.

Gradually as the years trooped by, we achieved the modern comforts, one by one—with improvements—but we never quite caught up with Charlie Erbe's folks, for Mr. Erbe became the head of a big patent-medicine firm and by the time we had electric lights, a shower bath, a screened-in porch and a connected icebox with tiled lining, the Erbes were living in one of the most elaborate mansions in town.

Only Charlie had no parties at the new home. He died of scarlet fever less than two months after the visit I have described.

The White
and the Beautiful

Snow in our town was something to await with great eagerness. Whether it was that first home-made sled that Pa had so proudly constructed or the shiny, yellow and red Flexible Flyer with glistening steel runners that came later, you hauled it out and belly-whopped down the steep hill. At the bottom was a snow-pile, not too white and not too soft, but only a sissy would shy away from it. You were supposed to drive right smack into it. It was such fun as I've probably never had since.

Then I learned something. There were still greater thrills that came with the possession of a sled. You tied it behind one of the big brewery trucks and just let it carry you on and on, block after block. Once when I felt I had traveled too far from home, I tried to untie the rope but couldn't. I had to cling on until we arrived at the brewery, where, being too young to detect twinkles in the eye, I believed the driver when he told me the sled was now a permanent fixture of his truck and that if I ever so much as uttered a cry, he would turn me over to the police. But I wanted that sled. So I whimpered. Whereupon the driver and his helper both made faces and frowned and finally one said, all right, if I would drink a glass of beer all the way down without stopping for breath, I could have the sled.

I nodded a reluctant assent and the helper came out with the beer. I drank it—a few gulps, that is—and could go no further. I was seven or eight, and it was my first taste of beer. I didn't like it, but I got my sled. I have had a great deal of beer since, but have never drunk it for such a worthy cause.

There were years when Winter meant snow—snow that stayed for weeks and piled itself high in front of our house. Those mysterious and also ludicrous contraptions we called "automobubbles" were beginning to appear on the streets, but you never saw a sign of them in the season of snow. No, sir! People rode in sturdy sleighs driven by one or two healthy horses. The little bells jingled gayly; steam plumed from the nostrils of the trotting nags; and the soft thuds of their hoofs on the blanketed ground were muffled drum beats. The big event was the day your pa proudly announced he had hired a sleigh for the day from Milton's stables—with two horses. He was going to drive, of course, but somewhere along the route you knew you could wheedle him into letting you control the reins for a spell.

You belonged to the gang on Locust Street. There was also a gang on Cooke Street. There was snow—nice, clean, damp snow. There must be a battle. Your heartaches were many because you never were picked as the leader. At best you were occasionally an under-lieutenant directing the squad which packed the snowballs for ammunition. You erected barriers and a conical tower into which a flag was stuck. Your gang waited patiently for the foe to start firing first because it was an established fact that the first side to commence hostilities would lose. So you'd probably both begin firing together. Occasionally some genius had the brilliant idea of dipping the snowball into water and when it froze—look out! To slip a piece of coal in as a core was unethical, it was dirty, but we were from eight to fourteen then and ethics was something learned in spelling lessons.

When you were licked, you were supposed to substitute a white handkerchief for the flag. That was a sign of submission. The afternoon wore on. The sun slunk down behind the hills. Night came on. But neither side ever stuck up that white flag.

You woke up on a December morning, and, look, the yard was covered with the white, the beautiful snow. Your teacher had told you each flake was a distinctly formed crystal, a beautiful piece of lace work. She implored you to study it under a magnifying glass. But who wanted to study snow? Snow was something with which to build human caricatures. Snow was something with which to build odd-shaped huts.

You and your buddies gathered it for the sculptural masterpiece. You rolled a snowball until it reached huge proportions; then you flattened it and oblonged it into a huge lozenge. Two of them were the legs. Or if you were of the modernistic school you simply scooped out a narrow ridge in a snow base you had built; that was enough to indicate the legs. You patted out two thinner and longer lozenges. The arms. Now a large and fat one—that was the torso. And then the head. You jabbed two holes near the forehead. You stuck coal into them, and eyes gleamed out darkly at you. A piece of wood made an ideal nose. You ran a line of coal chips over the chin, and a mouth grinned. A snowman alone was a dismal sight. He should have something to guard. A snowhouse. You made a great big heap. You flattened and patted it with the back of your shovel. Then you dug the opening and shelled it out. When it was completed, you crawled in, and you were an Eskimo! The thrill of the great bleak open North was yours. True, you had no sealskin boots, no bearskin gauntlets, and fish fat would sicken you, but you were an Eskimo, fast and secure in your igloo.

There was that day when six of you fastened your sleds together into a loosely joined toboggan and went whizzing down the icy hill. It was a terrifying experience, the first time, but nothing went wrong, and thereafter it was a thrilling ride, but without fear.

The white symmetry of a tree with the soft ermine over its branches, the song of feet crunching into the ice-brittled snow in the quiet of night, the tapestry of slant and flat roofs covered with the white fleece—these were charms of winter that made no impression until they were recalled in later years.

Snow—and a Woman

Snow laid its soft fragrant linen over the city and it was white and it was beautiful and comforting under foot. Near the entrance of the Belasco Theatre where young Mr. Clifford Odet's new play, Rocket to the Moon, was having its premiere, a sullen-eyed woman in a threadbare coat and slippers worn thin stopped the gay, chattering theatregoers, one by one.

She made no request, nor uttered word of any kind. She merely placed a hand on elbows of passers-by, stared into faces, and did not change expression as she was thrust aside.

The snow swirled as in those old-fashioned, water-filled crystal balls we used to shake, and most of us buttoned our coats more snugly and hastened into the warm lobby, but the woman stood there, unblinking, staring into each face—as if in search.

And when we came out, hours later, she was still there. And now the snow had climbed to the hem of her skirt and fleeced her lashes, but in her eyes was still the sullen misery.

And somehow, it seemed to me that here was a face I once knew, and I associated it with gayety and music and dancing —and the stage.

But I did not stop and ask her who she was, nor what it was she seemed to be seeking, for the snow was blinding me and now it was cold, bitter snow from which I wanted to flee to refuge in some nice, warm, lively café.

CHAPTER FOUR

Grandpa's Store

I walked up Grand Avenue recently, but the grocery store my grandpa ran was no longer there. The building has been remodeled and now there is a glittery hardware store and a dream of a pharmacy next door. Even the undertaking parlor is gone, replaced by a restaurant.

My fine old Jewish Grandpa had his grocery store when there were no nickelodions in the neighborhood and saloons had swinging doors, under which we used to peek to get a glimpse of lurid paintings of buxom nudes. A trip to Grandpa's store was a treat. Grandma always gave me a piece of chocolate and let me take a free chance on the chocolate Easter eggs. There was a bundle of cardboard slips and you pulled one out. If you drew Number One you received the biggest egg of all, with fancy icing. Once I did pull Number One but Grandpa chided Grandma for handing me the prize egg and she persuaded me to give it back to her.

The big excitement was behind the counter. My grandparents didn't go in for wrapping bundles with fancy white or yellow paper. They bought loads of old newspapers and stored them under that counter. Grandpa was very deft in wrapping a loaf of bread or dried mackerel. He did it so you always had a neat headline on top. I spent many hours in back of that counter going through the newspapers. Always I managed to locate the prize trove—the funnies.

I wasn't much of a reader in those days, but I could, with a great deal of effort, spell out and sound the important words in the little balloons, provided they weren't longer than one syllable. So I managed to follow the adventures of Happy Hooligan and Gloomy Gus, Buster Brown and Mary Jane, Little Nemo, Foxy Grandpa, the Katzenjammer Kids and others of that unforgettable crew in color. I squatted down in the shadows behind the long counter and lived with these erratic but lovable folk of the comics and had day dreams of meeting some day the wonderful and beautiful Lady Bountiful who was always giving away things or with Gaston and Alphonse who were so impressively polite.

Years later I met the creator of Lady Bountiful, Gene Carr, but became more friendly with his lovely wife, who had divorced him, and their daughter, an exquisite beauty, named Cleanthe, who is an exceptional painter and caricaturist and one of whose rare etchings is among my prized possessions.

And one day, there dropped out of the mail a letter from Carl E. Schultze, who had conceived those delightful strips detailing the adventures of kindly old "Foxy Grandpa." I had believed him long dead, as did many others, for when I mentioned in my column that in his letter he confessed he was eking out a bare existence drawing posters for a Y.M.C.A. branch, I was deluged with notes from readers, asking what they could do to help the fine old artist back on his feet.

One morning the mail brought a card with a drawing

of the round-faced, rosy-cheeked Foxy Grandpa as I remembered him from those other days, with a grinning rabbit leaning against his shoulder and this inscription: "To Louis Sobol, my friend. A smile from Foxy Grandpa and his little old Bunny. So nice to be alive with nice people who are alive. So Happy Days. Carl E. Schultze."

It reached me on January 19, 1939. That afternoon, the newspapers carried the announcement of the death of my friend. Almost within the hour when his card had reached me.

Once, inspired by some reckless impulse, Grandpa permitted me to wait upon a customer. The purchase was a loaf of bread—that I do remember—and I wrapped it up myself, but my disappointment was keen when the woman handed me the exact amount. I had wanted to make change. There was a reason for that.

Grandpa had no hifalutin cash register. The money was kept in a drawer with little compartments in back of the counter. You pressed a tiny knob and the drawer sprang out and a little bell rang.

Also Grandpa's system of bookkeeping was quite simple —to him, but not to me. He used an abacus. It was a pleasure to watch the deftness and rapidity with which he did his addition and subtraction, sliding the wooden balls up and down on their wires.

There came another great day. A soda fountain was installed. Nothing was more fascinating than watching Grandpa push down a plunger and see the chocolate or vanilla or lemon syrup squirt into the glass. Another lever siphoned the dancing, bubbly soda water. A scoop of ice cream and a little stirring with a long spoon, and there was that delectable luxury—an ice-cream soda.

In those days, Grandpa didn't believe in the extravagance of straws. You drank your soda from the glass after each spoonful of ice cream.

It was many months before Grandpa permitted me to fix up my first ice-cream soda. Only once, though, for I made such a mess of it, he never again allowed me near the precious fountain.

He was extremely religious—always reading from his huge Bible and repeating from it out loud—sometimes with a hum. One late afternoon, when he was alone in the store, two hoodlums entered and demanded his cash. Grandpa was frightened. He began screaming the names of the Prophets. The invaders, convinced he must be calling to his sons in back of the store, fled in alarm.

Grandpa died at seventy-eight and Grandma gave up the grocery store. One morning she didn't wake up either. She was eighty although she always said she would live to be 100 because her mother died at ninety-six and her grandmother at ninety-two.

Dogs

There were plenty of dogs in our neighborhood, but there never was one in our house—for long. Not because we didn't like dogs. As a matter of fact, my father was always saying the house ought to have a dog, but he knew we would never get around to really owning one.

There was a reason for that. It was because of my mother.

She loved pets. There was always a cat around the place and a canary, but it was different with dogs. Not that she loved them less, but because she had such a tender heart.

On two occasions, my father brought home a cute puppy. Always handy with tools, he had first built a kennel in the cellar without telling my mother, and although she may have noticed that there was some active carpenter work being done, it never occurred to her, I guess, that Pa was building a dog house.

At any rate, he came home from work one night with the tiny pup—a cocker-spaniel. My mother took it from him and snuggled the little fellow up against her cheek and cried: "Look at the itsy, witsy itta baby. Is it a pwecious itta baby?"

My sister, who was about two, reached her hands up, appealing for the pet, but my mother said, "No. It's too small. You'll drop it."

My sister started to cry. Mama said, "All right, darling, pet it. Just pet it," and my sister was appeased.

Later my father broke down and confessed he had already built a kennel and we all went downstairs into the cellar to put the puppy to bed. We had named it "Shnook."

Well, there we were down in the cellar to put "Shnook" to bed when my mother suddenly snatched him and said, no, such a baby couldn't be left alone in the dark, dark cellar. He would sleep in the bedroom. On the rug.

My father, disappointed because his doghouse was being spurned, said that wouldn't be wise, and he explained why.

My mother giggled and said, "That's right. I never thought of that. Little Shnookie, he's a baby with no didies. Just a baby."

So my father brought up a box from the cellar and my mother stuffed an old cushion into it. Shnookie who had been very quiet, except for an occasional whine, was placed snugly in it and we stood around and watched him close his eyes and go to sleep.

I don't know what time it was that I became aware of a wailing. It woke me up. I heard my father and mother talking to each other in their bedroom. Shnookie was crying bitterly. It was a heartbreaking crying, too—sobs and whines, then long wails.

I ran into my parents' bedroom. My mother had Shnookie in her arms, cuddled, but he was still whimpering. My father looked cross. He delivered an ultimatum, and a few minutes later the puppy was downstairs in the little kennel.

There was quiet for five minutes. Then up came the wails again. It was like a child's crying. There were voices again in the next bedroom, and then I saw my mother going to the door that led to the cellar. A few seconds later she was back with Shnookie in her arms.

I fell asleep shortly after that but I learned the next morning she had walked the floor with the puppy all night. Every time she let him out of her arms, he bawled.

That evening, when my father came home, my mother told him it was no use. It was heartbreaking, she said, to take a little dog away from its mother. He must take it back. Maybe, when Shnookie was a few months older, we could have him again. My father said that was silly. You had to break in a dog early in life to win his real affection.

Several years later, Pa again brought home a puppy, and again we went through the harrowing experience. That settled it—once and for all. We never had a dog again until I had a home of my own and acquired a wirehaired pup named "Whiskey" who achieved a bit of fame around Broadway, but that's another story.

But there were plenty in the neighborhood. There was no talk of prize winners and fancy breeds and dog shows. They were just plain hounds without any airs about them, but they were lovable and loyal and I envied their owners.

I remember particularly an old ferocious-looking bulldog, the only dog I can remember ever having feared during my boyhood days. Actually, he only looked tough; he really was a gentle fellow who wanted nothing much except to be permitted to sleep unmolested under the great elm directly in front of the Shannahan's house, where he lived. That dog slept most of the day and most of the night. We would shout "Bubbles" (his silly name), and he would open one eye, look over at us wearily, close it and slumber on.

One day the Shannahans took Bubbles to a relative's farm near Woodmont, Conn., and shortly afterward we learned the sad news. The genial, sleepy bulldog was dead.

And such an odd death for the fine old fellow. Bubbles had taken his snooze under a big tree in one of the fields. No one knows exactly how or why it happened, but he came scrambling in a frenzy to the farmhouse with hundreds of bees clinging to him and stabbing him.

The bees were chased off (George Shannahan was stung, though) and then poor Bubbles' wounds were dressed. But evidently an infection had set in. He was dead the following morning.

Earning an Easy Buck

A fellow, crowding along eleven or twelve, could lure some neat change for himself in those days. For one thing, snow fell more often, and thicker. The competition was fairly keen, but an enterprising lad who wasn't afraid to walk up and ring a doorbell and inquire politely: "Want your sidewalk cleaned, Ma'am?" could and would do all right.

Personally, I preferred to team up with a buddy who could deliver the sales talk. Our fee ran anywhere from fifteen to as much as thirty-five cents, depending upon the cement acreage to be cleared. We were not too haughty about it, however, if our employer said a dime and no more. In that case, the job was completed for a dime, though we might leave a fringe of snow here and there, merely out of principle and to indicate our protest at having our set rates slashed. Often we split equal shares of as much as $1—sometimes $1.50.

But there were other sources of income. Some of us were fortunate enough to be chosen to deliver a throwaway weekly newspaper. The pay was $1.50, and each of us had his own route. We spent an hour or two filling in the inserts at the printing plant; then off we went to make the deliveries from door to door. I quickly acquired the knack of folding and tossing, which saved climbing many porch steps.

It fell to my lot to make the delivery to the Jolly Boys' Club—60 papers in all. Naturally, this meant I had less homes to cover, less territory to roam. In one fell swoop, I was able to dispose of almost one-third of my weekly cargo.

It was a short-lived triumph. A half dozen of my estimable confreres crowded around me one afternoon, a short distance from the plant, tore my bag of papers from me and then proceeded to pummel the daylights out of me.

"Smart guy," they jeered. One after another rubbed my nose in the dirt, punched me, kicked me, dragged me along the ground and inflicted other indignities. In a piece of fiction, I should have risen and fought them off. I didn't. I picked up the bruised remains and walked home, reflecting bitterly on the general injustice prevalent in this none-too-happy world.

There were some thoughts of revenge, but they were all in the mind. I saw myself meeting each of my assailants and knocking the stuffings out of him. As he lay on the ground, pleading for mercy, I would warn him that he might expect the same treatment every time I ran across him. That went, too, for all the rest. I saw myself being regarded with awe—in the school yard, in the play fields, on the streets. People buzzed in awe as I passed by. Most of my great victories and conquests have been day dreams.

I never went back to my paper route.

Two doors away from where we lived was a wonderfully kind old man who had a horse and wagon and sold fruits and vegetables. He would walk alongside his horse, shouting, "Sterrr-owbries" or "Warrr-malll'ns" and the housewives would stick their heads out of the windows or else come out wiping their hands on their aprons. The wares would be inspected, the deal consummated. This wonderfully kind old man would pay an ambitious boy fifty cents to help him out on a Saturday. You met him all ready to set out, at the stable three blocks away, about 9 in the morning and by 5 in the afternoon, sometimes even 4:30, you were through. And for that—all of half a dollar!

When the milkman's son was sick, which was often, your mother would say: "Mr. Cutler wants to know do you want to help out washing the bottles," and you would rush over after school and put in two or three hours, plucking the bottles out of tubs of hot, soapy water, running a brush around the inside of their bellies, piling them into the wooden crates.

But the real fun was putting on the caps. Mr. Cutler would always fill the milk bottles himself, never trusting hired help with that precious and delightful task, but for consolation, you were permitted to slap on those little round cardboard covers.

Mr. Cutler generously paid me fifty cents for only three hours' work, and there was one week, after I had put in seven days' labor, when he made it $4 even. As additional reward I rode out to the country with him occasionally, sometimes as far as Milford. Mr. Cutler often would let me handle the reins myself.

In summer, some of the more opulent neighbors would oblige a young fellow by letting him sweep their sidewalks, which, they told him, they could do just as well themselves, but if he would do that, mow the lawn, water it and perhaps run an errand or two—well, all right, you do that and we'll see. There was no advance bargaining. Sometimes you drew a nickel—sometimes fifteen cents. But it added up.

There were days, too, when word was spread that certain delightful if strange gentlemen were practically throwing their money away, offering $1 to each boy who would take a bagful of circulars or sample pills and distribute them from door to door. This was a soft touch, and a great occasion always.

Once, gentlemen of this class had us distribute little packets, each containing two chocolate-covered confections. Unfortunately they did not take the precaution to warn us not to experiment with the little samples. Several of us, thus unwarned, ate a great many of them and found them quite palatable. The results, later that evening, however, were less than pleasant, although no doubt highly salutary.

At any rate, a chap of ten or twelve or thereabouts, on the lookout, encountered little trouble gathering in spending money, nor was there much trouble getting rid of it. For a nickel, you could enjoy a marvelous ice-cream sundae with chocolate or strawberry or cherry sauce with ground nuts, or if you were profligate enough to splurge, a dime would get you a banana split with two big balls of ice cream, a whole strawberry or cherry on each delicious mound, flanked by slit, gorgeous bananas.

A thick disc of apple pie or peach pie was a nickel.

Lemon, orange or vanilla soda was two cents, three cents or a nickel, depending upon the place you patronized. There was a nice candy—the name of which I have forgotten—which cost only a penny. With each one came a small card bearing the picture of a baseball player, Indian chief, actress or President. These you traded with other collectors. Some were extremely rare. You might have to turn in as many as ten actresses to get the coveted Geronimo or Andrew Jackson.

Hokey-pokey wagons were always near the school, offering an oblong of brick ice cream for a penny or two cents. Ice-cream sandwiches were a penny. Snowballs—shaved ice saturated with a heavenly liquid flavor—lemon, orange or raspberry, usually cost as much as two to three cents.

In between times, you added to your personal possessions such amazing bits of property as a magic lantern with a dozen slides or a Flexible Flyer with lightning runners or real ball-bearing roller skates. It was simple. You sold twenty-four packets of blueing or bars of soap and sent the money back to the company, and within two weeks you would have the magic lantern or the sled or the skates.

One day I went into business for myself. A boy up the block was moving out of the neighborhood and his father approached mine—and the deal was closed. For $25, I had an enterprise which yielded $6.30 a week. A newspaper route. The understanding was that I was to pay the $25 back to my father at the rate of $5 a week. Thereafter the $6.30 was to be mine, but there were still conditions. Five dollars were to be banked weekly.

The first four or five months of my business career were thrilling. There was the satisfaction of knowing, as I lined up to receive my papers at the window in the circulation

74

department, that I was my own boss. I could come late if I wished or not at all if I were that indiscreet. As a matter of record, I usually arrived early.

The paper I handled was folded peculiarly. I cannot recall, in all the years since, any other newspaper folded in that fashion. Instead of the customary single lap-over, our bright little hometown gazette had a doublefold, so that it came to the subscriber in a compact oblong. I must say it made for easier reading—and the truth is that unconsciously many of us today take our papers and fold them just that way for convenience.

Our newspaper was first folded lengthwise so that the whole right length of the paper was visible, and then folded again from top to bottom, leaving the upper right half exposed. I still think for large-sized newspapers this is as practical a way of presenting a paper to the customer as any devised, although I suppose the publishers of tabloids will point proudly to their own improvement.

However, to us young distributors, it wasn't the reading efficiency that impressed so much as the ease with which we could "cudgel" the paper: give it that bit of bend that made hurling it to the porch such simple pleasure. Sometimes, just to provide a variation, a fellow would "scale" the paper, without even bothering to roll or bend it.

As months went by, I added to my business—new customers moving in—or by purchasing small routes, until one day I discovered I couldn't carry my bag of papers, so heavy had the load become. A few days later, I became an employer. I hired a kid from our neighborhood at a weekly salary of $1.50. Since he was larger, though younger, I consigned most of the weight to him and suddenly learned the pleasure in being boss. You could get the other fellow to do most of the work.

I don't think I did any serious pondering over this

acquirement of a new social status, but gradually I fell more and more into the habit of letting young Jimmy Carrington do the work while I lingered in the ice-cream parlors.

Then came the time when I hired my second assistant, Jimmy's brother, Henny. To the young Carringtons, I turned over the distribution and confined myself to the collections, which took me over the course twice a week. Some customers paid on Mondays, others on Fridays.

Only when Christmas was approaching did I take renewed interest in my business. I went along with Jimmy one day—with Henny the other—even flung a paper or two. About three days before Christmas, I shoved little greeting cards I had bought at the five-and-ten into every paper.

The loot was terrific, and I am pleased to recall that I had the good grace to share the swag with my "employees."

Then one day Jimmy was bedded with a cold and I had to take over. A few days later, Henny was down with pneumonia. So I had the entire route on my hands. Unfortunately, I had acquired a taste for loafing. To have to go out in the cold, blistery Connecticut afternoons, through freeze and blizzards, was something that distressed me woefully.

Without consulting my father, I sold the route—for $35. I thought it was a smart deal—$10 profit—but my father pointed out later that in addition to the $25 I had paid for the original business, I had expended about $30 in buying up smaller routes. He also did a bit of figuring for me, showing that a business yielding between $12 and $13 weekly was an idiotic giveaway at $35. In brief, my father made it plain that I was a fool.

Lost Opportunity

I stood in line with others just out of uniform. We were in the large, barren-looking chamber of the old Health Building, set aside as a government employment bureau for ex-service men. It was the summer of 1919—and I was out of a job. I need not have been. A few months previously I had eloped with a red-headed girl and had decided the $24 a week I was earning as acting city editor of a Waterbury, Conn., newspaper was totally inadequate, especially in view of the promise held forth in the great Metropolis, where men, so it was reported, were drawing down as high as $50 a week as reporters—$100 a week as salesmen.

No newspaper in New York seemed too eager for my services. I had been a dismal failure as (1) a salesman for a paper drinking-cup company; (2) an advertising solicitor for a theatrical weekly; (3) a telephone salesman for a stock and bond house in Wall Street.

So here I was in the old Health Building, waiting my turn. The young men and women were courteous and apparently eager to be helpful. They assisted us in filling out applications; they interviewed us; they made suggestions as to the type of work we should seek.

Finally, I was given a card with an address and a name. The prospect needed a secretary and evidently I possessed the essential qualifications. It was suggested I speed out to his home in Brooklyn forthwith and present myself for the position.

I stepped outside—and the rains came. I can't remember that it had ever rained so hard in New York or in Connecticut. This was a deluge—a flood from the skies. I had no umbrella, no raincoat, no rubbers. Brooklyn seemed so very far away. Besides I was depressed. Rain always depresses a man out of a job.

I went to a movie instead. Heaven knows I had very little money to squander, yet I indulged in this needless extravagance—25 cents for a seat at the movies. It was not a good movie—that I can recollect—and I felt guilty as I headed home to our furnished room to tell my bride that the day had been fruitless, but that there was a promise of a job. I was going to look into it the following day. I did not tell her that instead of following up the lead promptly I had gone to the picture show instead.

There was bright sun and warmth outside the following morning. It was a day to lift the spirits of a young bridegroom who had so recklessly abandoned a good job to try his luck in the big city. I rode out to Brooklyn in the subway and finally found myself in front of the address marked on my card. It was a neat two-story house with a patch of front yard. I ran up the short flight of porch steps and rang the doorbell eagerly.

I waited a few seconds—and rang again. I might have still been there, futilely pressing that button, if a next-door neighbor hadn't stuck her head out of the window.

"They've gone," she said, "They'll be away for a couple of months, the whole summer I guess. They've gone to Birmingham. That's where they've gone. You know, in Alabama."

Disconsolately, I inquired, "When did they go?"

"Oh, they left about 9 o'clock this morning. I guess they won't be back for a couple of months."

With a sinking heart I walked toward the subway station. I had muffed my chance of becoming the secretary to an author whose stories I had admired—Octavus Roy Cohen.

CHAPTER FIVE

The Roomer

Occasionally, we had a lodger for the spare room. In our neighborhood, a family could take in a roomer and still mingle gracefully, proudly, with friends and relatives.

Most of the neighbors took in roomers, and, in fact, up the street, the Donderos, who had the big house with the twin maples in front and who celebrated with a grand party every year when the grape-pressing period in the cellar was over, had seven lodgers. A few of them doubled up. They were great-hearted folks, the Donderos, and when a homeless Italian came to town and was recommended to them, they didn't have the heart to say no. When you consider that the Donderos themselves were nine in the family and that the house contained only ten rooms in all, you must admit they were hospitable people to put up with all that crowding.

In our own case, we had only two roomers in all the time I can remember—one at a time, of course. The first one is very dim in my memory, but the second remained with us for more than two years and my recollection of him and his genial eccentricities will never vanish. I always pictured him as someone quite elderly, but recently, in discussing him with my parents, I learned he was only thirty-two or thirty-three when first he came to live with us.

He was a Russian who had been a Count—a real Count. His name was Grigor. My father had brought him home one night and asked my mother if she would let him have the spare room for a couple of weeks until he located a permanent home. He stayed with us for two years.

As a boy his hobby had been watches. Ripping them apart and assembling them again was his chief pleasure. Now he had arrived in our town and obtained a job in the watch factory, assigned to the department which was bossed by my father. Pa, who was always partial to people who had suffered or had romantic backgrounds, took a fancy to this tall Russian whose English was often unintelligible.

Grigor had been messed up in something political in St. Petersburg and had fallen out of favor with the Czar, whose police set out to arrest him. He told the story often. Arrest meant Siberia. Siberia was a dread, ice-bound, blizzardy place where people worked in mines and were whipped with something called a knout. While I shivered with delight, Grigor told me that after a man was beaten by the whips, salt was rubbed into his wounds.

This made less impression than you might think. I could not understand why rubbing salt in raw places was so uncomfortable. I cannot recall that my spirit of curiosity ever tempted me to have a confederate use his whip and rub salt in my open wounds. It was the way Grigor described the painful process that brought goose-pimples.

In our neighborhood, a lodger paid anywhere from $2 weekly to perhaps as much as $5. Grigor insisted upon handing my mother $3 a week, and for that, in addition to a nice, large room with two windows, he had his breakfast with us—stewed prunes, oatmeal, two-soft-boiled eggs, bread and butter and cocoa and my mother's jam. Of course, coffee, as I've told you, was taboo. There came a day when Grigor inquired timidly whether it would be too much trouble to have tea for breakfast? Thereafter that's what he got.

On Sundays, the Count had dinner with us at 1 o'clock, and occasionally during the week, he sat down for supper. Every Friday he brought home a bagful of fruit for my mother and often he would run to the corner and return with a quart of ice cream. Once he bought me a Flexible Flyer, and on another occasion, for my sister, who was just past two, a huge doll which squealed "Ma-ma" if you tipped her over.

The $3 he paid for his weekly room rent was my mother's exclusive loot. She banked it in her little teapots or vases.

There came dark depression days. One afternoon my father announced grimly that the shop had closed down and he was out of a job. Later Grigor came home, too. Although it wasn't Friday, he had two big bags of fruit and a bag containing cakes. We all sat down and had a party, and my mother brought out wine to celebrate the bad news.

Grigor, who stayed on with us without paying, went out daily, looking for work. My father, on the other hand, had written several letters, and shortly after I heard the exciting news. We were moving back to New Haven. But Grigor was not going. Later I learned my mother had gone to him with practically all the money he had paid her for room rent—money which she had carefully saved—and had handed it to him.

Grigor protested. Finally she got my father to speak

to him—and Pa pleaded with him to take at least half of it. Grigor yielded, and everyone was happy.

The following morning, though, there was no sign of the Count. On his bureau my mother found a brief note, thanking her and my father for their kindness. The note was wrapped around the money she had given him—all but $10. He left no clue to his destination.

Then one day, many months later, a letter came and in it $10. It had been sent to our Greenville house and was forwarded from there. The postmark was Buffalo, N.Y., but Grigor wrote nothing about how he had gotten there or what he was doing. Nor was there a return address.

The Tooth Will Out

A fellow didn't lose prestige in our neighborhood if he made an appearance in public with a tooth or two missing in front.

Somehow there always was a tooth or two that was loose, and, following a custom which prevailed from coast to coast, the ceremony of extraction was often quite simple. If you wanted to be dramatic, you tied a string around it, fastened the other end to a door and with the co-operation of an eager confederate—zip! ouch!—and it was over. You bled quite satisfactorily and rushed to your mother, who, after scolding you, made you rinse your mouth with salt water and gave you a penny as solace. And a kiss.

Another dramatic extraction of a loose tooth—and sound one—was effected by methods not often recommended. The thing to do was to toss a few words of opprobrium at the neighborhood bully—or a stick or stone. We had no bully, but a fellow named Schindler used to do a lot of fighting. He was hot-tempered. He wasn't much bigger than the rest of us, nor any older, but there was no one his age or weight and over he couldn't or wouldn't lick when the occasion demanded.

I never had a fight with Schindler because I was scared to death of him. In fact, I was pretty much a sissy when it came to getting into a scrap. But once Schindler was showing us a new exercise they were taking up in the school gym, and, during the demonstration, the back of his hand pounded accidentally against my mouth. That's when I learned how simple it was to lose a tooth even when you weren't looking.

I had one large incisor in front, however, that was as firm and apparently as permanent as the Rock of Gibraltar. Since my second teeth were pushing up, it was evident something of an impasse was inevitable because of that stubborn front one. Finally, it was decided at a conference of my elders that this was a case for the dentist.

There had been some talk among the boys about the sadistic orgies that took place in the dens of torture operated by the dentists. Added to that, old Dr. Fleischner, who did most of the work in our neighborhood, was a grouchy, formidable-looking gentleman. My mother had made the mistake once or twice, in earlier years, of threatening to take me to Dr. Fleischner if I didn't behave.

Now my doom was at hand. I tried to forestall it by resorting to the string-and-pull method, but I was slightly older and more timid now. My father and mother cheered me up. They said it was nothing—absolutely nothing. The dentist would tell me to open my mouth and close my eyes. Then a second later I would open my eyes and close my mouth and that would be all. The tooth would be out.

I didn't quite understand how that could be, and my folks were vague about it, but utterly confident and optimistic and light-hearted. So the fateful day came. I had to go through with it because all that week I had confided to the fellows in the neighborhood, to the girls and boys in my class and finally to my teacher that I was going to have my tooth pulled. I wanted sympathy in advance and also, perhaps, a fragment of appreciation for my impending heroism. I don't recall that anyone was impressed.

Whether dentists used anesthesia and anodynes in those days, I don't know. Grouchy old Doc Fleischner evidently didn't believe in those hifalutin pain-killers. Nor did he make any pretense of being sympathetic and kindly. He put on no act as dentists do these days to encourage timorous patients.

Old Doc Fleischner growled and h-r-rumphed as he stared into my open mouth, grunted something about too much candy and snarled. "Sit still. Keep your mouth open. Wider! Wider!! What's the matter—can't you open your mouth?"

My mother held my hand tightly and I began wondering whether anything could be done to a fellow who slid out of a dentist's chair and ran away. Then suddenly the old doc thrust a horrifying instrument into my mouth and the next second I felt an awful tug and twist of the tooth and such excruciating pain as I've never known since.

Don't tell me that pulling out a first tooth is as painless and easy as plucking a pin from a cushion. I yelled, then whimpered, and have been frightened of dentists ever since.

Old Doc Fleischner relaxed and said I had been pretty brave, after all, and he was going to give me a present. He went into the other room and came back quickly and handed me a little box, something like those little jewelers' boxes for rings. It was wrapped neatly. Doc Fleischner said not to open it until I got home.

My mother paid him his fee—$1—said something about coming around to see him next week, and we went home. Every time we met someone we knew, I opened my mouth and showed the result of the operation.

At home I could scarcely wait to open the little box. There, nestling like a warped pearl dipped in ketchup, was my tooth!

Minor Thrills

To repeat, the thrills for a young fellow were simple and inexpensive and innocent. There was no swing. This was before the Alexander's Ragtime Band era—no rug-cutting, jitterbugging, reefer-smoking. On the other hand there were no laws making it obligatory for an adult to accompany a youngster to a movie house.

The vaudeville and films at the Bijou were changed twice a week and if you were fortunate enough to possess one of those coupons—and somehow you most always were—it cost only ten cents for three hours of diversion.

I must explain about those coupons. When you bought an original ticket of admission to the orchestra, the cost, if I recall, was thirty cents. But attached was the "coupon," so that the next time you went to the Bijou, you only had to pay ten cents along with the free ticket. Naturally, these bits of pasteboard were highly valued among us (and among the adults, too, for that matter) and frequently we used them as a medium of exchange. Some of the boys, by hook or crook, would manage to collect dozens of the precious coupons, and sell them or use them for barter.

That Bijou was a theatre of imposing grandeur. Its

rococo lobby was positively breath-taking, but the architectural *pièce de resistance* was the glass stairs through which water tumbled in the colors of the rainbow. That beautiful water and its changing hues were a mystery that was not solved until years later, when you realized it was all done with lights.

Now that I look back, the Bijou was small-time; the Big Time was across the street at Poli's. There were four shows daily at the Bijou—five minor acts and the full-length silent picture. At the more exclusive Poli's there were usually eight acts—but no picture—and only two shows a day. It was at Poli's, that I first became acquainted with the great art of Jimmy Hussey, Sophie Tucker, Phil Baker and Ben Bernie, George Jessel, Eva Tanguay, Nora Bayes and others of that illustrious tribe, living and dead.

But some of our biggest stars of today weren't too proud to play in the less important Bijou, even though four shows daily meant a certain loss of face.

Another minor thrill was provided by our neighborhood drugstore. The pharmacies of our day, short-sightedly enough, sold only medicines and medical products, and the only books were those in which the druggist pasted up his prescriptions. Nowadays, you can't tell whether you're in a book store or an electrical-appliance bazaar.

Of course, there was one lure, which I've mentioned before: the marble soda fountain where a nickel produced a wonderful, tantalizing cherry college ice, and if you plunged to the extent of a dime you had a million calories served in the form of a banana split with two scoops of ice-cream.

The drug store we patronized had a monthly prize bag, and the boys and girls in the neighborhood looked forward to the day when the dividend was distributed. Every regular customer, purchasing fifty cents' worth of medical commodities on the appointed day, received the prize bag. It was filled to the top with everything imaginable, and the thrill was to run home and empty out the loot.

There would be sample tubes of toothpaste or cans of tooth or foot powder, a packet of seidlitz powders, a small package of gum, sample packets of every headache or stomach pill ever advertised. There would be a small chocolate bar, perhaps a tiny thermometer, a foot-rule, a tape measure, a stick of licorice. Occasionally there would be a coupon. Only once was I lucky enough to draw a bag with the prized coupon. It was redeemable for an ice-cream soda.

One day the drug store failed to open. I gathered by listening around that the nice, jolly, generous owner had been found dead in the back of the pharmacy and that it had not been a natural death. He had mixed up a poisonous potion and gulped it down. Most of us were too young to know what it was all about, but it appears he had been brooding for months over his wife, a middle-aged woman who had gone off with a drug salesman from Hartford.

When the store reopened three days later, the two clerks we knew were there, but it wasn't quite the same without the genial owner himself. A new pharmacist made his appearance about two weeks later, having bought the business from the errant widow. Though he tried to be pleasant, trade fell off. On top of that, he abandoned the practice of the free monthly prize bag, and gradually the folks in our neighborhood began to patronize a newer druggist two blocks away.

A fellow looked forward to Decoration Day, not from impulses of patriotism, but because it meant Savin Rock and White City were officially open for the season. They were our Coney Island and Atlantic City, our Palm Beach and Newport.

The wonders of Savin Rock and White City defy adjectival description. The breath-taking water and surface rides, the timorous invasion of the Old Mill, the reckless whirl on the carousel, the awe-inspiring trip through Fairyland, the hair-raising scoot down the water chute, the terrifying loop-the-loop dash, the savory candied apples on sticks, the hot dogs and iced lemonades, the Penny Arcade.

Many years later, I made a special trip back to Savin Rock. I wish I hadn't. The heavenly dreamland of my youth was just a tawdry little amusement park with cheapness etched all over its scabrous face. It was as if I had rushed eagerly to meet a beloved sweetheart of other years to find her a hard-bitten, blowsy streetwalker.

There was another minor boyhood thrill: fishing for killies. Killies are about the size of an anemic sardine, and evidently the greatest suckers on earth. A fellow never even had to use a hook to capture one. We simply tied a worm or part of a worm to the end of the line, and once the killy nibbled, he never let go until he was smack on the bank and in the can.

After we had caught a few hundred of them, we would sell them as bait to the hardier fishermen who went out after bigger game.

Gambling

The folks in our neighborhood didn't go in for heavy gambling. Old Schmidtzl, the grocer, who had been a sergeant in the Prussian Army and who insisted a scar on his left cheek was from a student duel (his wife said that was nonsense—Schmidtzie was a softie who fainted at the sight of blood) used to have pinochle sessions at his home two or three times a week. Sometimes in back of Sam

Spingold's cigar store the older men gathered for their pinochle and occasionally there were whispers that, after hours, there were some frenzied poker games for high stakes—quarter stud and half-dollar blind openers!

My father never knew one card from another. In later years, both my mother and I endeavored to teach him casino, but my father said, no, he wasn't interested in cards, for that matter, in any gambling. He didn't put on righteous airs and say it was sinful or that it led to a fellow's downfall, but he had known people who had lost their businesses and their homes and even their wives because of gambling.

Once a friend who worked with him in the shop, in a fit of generosity, presented him with an Italian lottery ticket. The high stake was $10,000, and there were other rewards down to $100. My father brought the ticket home and for the next week or so he and my mother would vie with each other in planning the things they were going to do with the $10,000 when they won it.

As the date of the announcement of the lottery award drew close, my mother had reached a point where she was insisting that, when the money arrived, at least $1,000 of it must go to the friend who had given the ticket to my father. She said that was the fair thing to do and that she would never be able to look anyone in the face if she were to take this money and not turn over part of it to the man who had been so kind as to make a gift of the ticket.

"Who said no?" demanded my father. "The minute the money arrives—right away, $1,000 goes to Joe. I'll take it to him in $10 bills. I'll count it out and I'll say, 'Joe, here is $1,000. Take it. It's yours. You are my friend—and this money is yours'."

Mama said, "Tomorrow when you're in the shop I want

you to tell Joe what we're going to do about the money. Tell him—the second it comes—it goes to him."

My father promised he would do that.

The results were announced. My father and mother were very blue indeed because not only did we not win the grand prize, but not even one of the small ones, not even a consolation of $100.

Pa's good humor saved the situation for him, softened the disappointment. If this had been an Irish lottery, he insisted, he would have won because he was always voting for Irishmen for Mayor and aldermen.

Mama, who thought all my father's little jokes extremely funny, giggled and then laughed.

As far as I know that was the nearest my father ever came to gambling, even though most of the men in our town bought those little lottery slips which paid off at that time, if I remember, 40 to 1, if your three numbers came up. There was a story going the rounds that one prominent member of our city administration had made a hit for $20,000, but, of course, the elders considered that mere scuttlebutt. A thin, dried-up, cold-eyed, old fellow named Sullivan was the Policy King. In later years he rode around in a huge Rolls Royce, the only one in town, and the legend (which nobody could prove) was that he gave away terrific sums for charity—but anonymously.

Not too many years ago I took Pa to a certain gambling house in New York and explained about the dice throwing and what the numbers on the green baize represented. He was interested in the roulette; he had seen moving pictures in which the wheel was featured. So I made him take a dollar chip from me and place it on a number, assuring him he would get back $35 worth of chips if the number came up.

"That number won't come up in a million years," said Pa. "Why should they let me put a dollar down and get back $35? What kind of business is that for them?"

The wheel turned, the little ball clicked into its notch— and Papa's number did not come up.

He smiled. "You see!" he said with an air of mild triumph. "Throwing money away."

My mother on the other hand was a great one for casino and in later years was initiated into poker by some of her woman friends. It was many months before she confessed to my father that the seventy cents she had won was the result of a phenomenal run at poker, and though it was after 10 o'clock at night, their bedtime, she wanted to sit down with him there and then and teach him the mysteries of the great American pastime. My father looked at her as if she were out of her mind, and the matter never came up again.

A year or so ago, when I was back home, visiting my folks, I learned my father had weakened and succumbed. Not to cards—he refuses to this day to learn the difference between a jack and a king—but to another game which, he confesses, he used to play many, many years ago, as a boy. Lotto.

One night a week at a different house each time, six couples gather, and, after the buffet, settle down to lotto, with prizes offered for those who fill their cards first.

My mother took me aside after my father had explained this to me. She whispered wickedly, "He thinks its lotto. It's bingo!"

The Duel

The night was cool and I was feeling beautiful when Mr. Toots Shor, the hash-house proprietor and well-known Volunteer Adviser to the White House and all points north, barged in. ("Barge" is a flat boat. Have you ever seen Mr. Shor's feet?)

Mr. Shor shouted, "What is this rumor, I hear, ya crumb bum, that you are the undisputed gin-rummy champeen of Greater New York as well as Hollywood?"

I replied softly, "That is not a rumor, Mr. Shor. That is a fact."

"Clear the tables," roared the Chronic Intruder. "Don't bother to get cards. I've brung my own. Hey, you, Sammy Renick, keep score. Low card deals. California—three across. Two extra boxes for gin—one for undercut. Name your price, ya phony, scribblin' hack."

"Penny," I said valiantly.

" 'Penny!' he sez, the cheap creep. 'Penny' he sez. Why, ya crumb bum, my bus boys play me for a nickel. Get me someone with fortitude. Wait'll I tell Hellinger, Sobol da champ wants I should play him for a penny. Hey, Ralph, get me Bob Hannegan on the phone. Yeah, in Washington. Try the White House. If the Prez answers, don't hang up. Tell him I gotta speak to Bob. Deal, ya bum!"

I shuffled. Mr. Shor cut. I dealt eleven cards to Mr. Shor, ten to myself. Mr. Shor deposited a queen of spades on the shiny table top. I ignored it, drew a card from the pack, boldly tossed out an ace of clubs, Mr. Shor hesitated. "An ace he throws! Brave man, he throws an ace. Me, I'm not so brave," jeered Mr. Shor. "Tootsie picks up the ace."

The phone rang. "Answer that, Sammy," ordered Mr. Shor, fumbling about with his cards. Mr. Renick answered.

92

"*The operator says Mr. Hannegan's secretary says Mr. Hannegan is not in,*" said Mr. Renick.

"*An ace he throws me,*" repeated Mr. Shor. "*What's the name o' the game?*"

He spread out his cards. The ace, added up to two in his hand, had given him gin, on the first pick! I said nothing. I did nothing. But my underlip began to bleed all of a sudden.

"*Put in a call for Sherman Billingsley,*" thundered Shor. "*Tell him his teacher's pet threw an ace and little Tootsie picked it up and went gin. Call the baron, Jack Kriendler. Tell him his champ has fainted from those steaks he feeds him on the cuff, da crumb bum, to get his name in the column. Me, Tootsie, I don't want my name in the column. I don't need my name in the column. Let him pay through the schnoz—pennies from Sobol's schnoz. Like a million dollars in the bank. Deal, little man, deal!*"

Silently, I shuffled, watched the cut, dealt. Mr. Shor dropped a king of clubs. I picked it up. I tossed a five of hearts. Mr. Shor spurned it, drew, laid down a ten of hearts. I picked it up and offered a nine of hearts.

"*Get that,*" sang Mr. Shor gaily. "*Two cards he picks up, brave little man. Takes a ten of hearts and gives me the nine. Got me buffaloed. Too smart for me. A regular Runyon —big league. Grabs a ten of hearts and gives me the nine. Tootsie isn't proud.*"

He reached for the phone. "*Sweetheart,*" he purred to the switchboard operator, "*get me Mark Hellinger—Hollywood, that's right, Hollywood. Then go over to Tiffany's and pick yourself out a little diamond bracelet. Sobol's compliments. Gin!*"

And he fanned out another killer.

"*Start countin', Champ!*" he commanded.

The phone rang. "*Mark, h're ya? Waddaya think I'm doin'? Wanna know? I'm beatin' the phony-baloney champ's*"

93

brains in. I got him against the wall and he's yellin' murder. I am blitzin' the champ. I've won half his crummy column already. Ya want a column cheap? I'll have it and all his stock in the paper in half an hour. When ya comin' East?"

The monologue went on endlessly and monotonously, while I counted up again. I had made no mistake. Plus his twenty-five for gin, I was handing Mr. Shor eighty-two points.

"Hellinger sez," advised Mr. Shor, "he'll be in New York in a couple of days. He sez drink a lotta milk and keep strong. He wants to take you on when he gets here."

I will spare you much of the painful details. Mr. Shor, the poor man's Escoffier, ginned and knocked and knocked and ginned until he had blitzed and murdered me into submission to the tune of 5,800 points in three series.

"Gotta leave ya now, has-been," said Mr. Shor. "Pay me by cash or by check—but get it up," said Mr. Shor. "I gotta write a note to my pal, Joe Nunan. I gotta tell him not to let me forget ta mark down my winnin's on my income-tax report. Study up on da game, ya crumb bum—and do me a favor—just like I asked Corum—keep my name out of da papers. Give those other Johnny-come-latelies the breaks— they need it—Billingsley, Kriendler, Lindy, Perona. Just play gin with me. I wanna move into a bigger apartment."

I sat quietly, unperturbed, completely master of myself. It is true, that like Nick the Greek on one occasion, when I took off my coat and rolled up my sleeves, there were finger-nail blue marks like a row of sapphires up the length of an arm. It is true the room seemed unusually hot and suddenly began to turn like a gyroscope.

But it was nothing—nothing at all.

I have now taken up a quiet little pastime known as parchesi, which I play with my wife.

CHAPTER SIX

=====

Shoes

The purchase of footwear in those days was never casual. Usually the entire family trooped downtown to the shoe-store, and we children sat by patiently while the older folks went into a weighty conference. If the shoes were for Pa, the deal might be concluded within fifteen minutes. It took much longer to please my mother.

The salesman, who was often the proprietor or his partner, would bring out the more expensive merchandise first, handling it delicately and affectionately.

"How much?" was the first question, even before examination.

"Well, to tell the truth," was the hesitant and somewhat uneasy reply, "these *are* a bit high, but, good gosh, they'll last a lifetime. Look how they shine . . ."

"How much?"

"We-e-ll, $5.50!"

"Five dollars and fifty cents!" Ma would exclaim, in a tone of dismay and rebuke. "Mr. Rapp, you must think we're rich millionaires like Rockefeller or something," and she would glance over at Pa. He would grin and come back with the joke he used for all shopping occasions:

95

"We didn't come in to buy the whole store, only a pair of shoes, Mr. Rapp."

Then Mr. Rapp would hold up a shoe, bend it slightly to reveal its flexibility, tug at the tongue, rub a handkerchief over the leather surface to demonstrate how quickly it took on a mirror gloss, and then, staring wistfully at his customers and detecting no sign of yielding, reluctantly put it aside, and grope about among the boxes for a less expensive make.

In those days, most of the folks in our neighborhood never thought of buying more than one pair of shoes a year for each member of the family. Occasionally, someone might splurge, if there'd been a windfall and when it was necessary to replace Sunday shoes which had worn out. But as a rule, the cobbler down the block got our business regularly.

The youngsters drew a better break than their elders because nature, which paid little attention to economics, saw fit to have their feet grow. Healthy kids were rough on their footgear, and even the most expert shoemaker would occasionally reach the point where he had to confess, in sturdy Sicilian accents, he could do no more patching.

A fellow on the way with his father and mother to buy a pair of shoes would conduct an eager and hopeful debate along the route. "Can I have patent leathers this time, Pa?" and Pa would reply, "In two days, with patent leathers the way you run around you would need another pair of shoes. Patent leathers crack." Your ma would try to soothe you by hinting that patent leathers might be all right for girls but for a chap practically a man and already in the fifth grade—well!

It was tough making up your mind, once in the shoe store. There was a dandy pair that buttoned up the sides. A hunkydory button-hook was a present with that particular set. Then there was a pair of low beautiful yellows like an egg's yolk, with leather shoe laces. Your father said how could you talk about wearing low shoes—with Winter practically here. When you got your first pair of long pants, that would be the time to consider low shoes.

Finally, you left with black, full shoes with wide round toes, having yielded happily because the folks were letting you walk home in them—and not saving them to wear later. Pa said not to mind the squeak because that would go away eventually.

Mind the squeak? What would new shoes mean without it? It was something to cherish, just like the souvenir that went with the shoes—a box of paints.

As a rule, though, the new shoes were something to put aside for Sunday and holiday use, at least for the first few weeks after the purchase. Then came the day when a fellow would wear them to school for the first time, feeling somewhat self-conscious, but a bit snobbish, too, and perhaps sorry for chaps who were still wearing their old mended ones.

That would be a day when he would remain stiffly aloof from the recess and after-school games—such as one o'cat, kick-ball, miggles, stump the leader or foot-races. Somehow, by the end of the day, the thrill of wearing those new shoes wasn't quite as keen. There was something about new shoes that kept a fellow from really being himself. It was a relief to get back into the old, battered pair—and be free again.

One of the first things to be done to shoes after a week or two was to have the cobbler nail metal taps shaped like quarter moons on the soles of the shoes and the back of the heels. This move was in the interest of sensible economy. It prevented the soles and heels from wearing down at the corners too rapidly. Of course, you couldn't move

97

along with the silence of a soft-pawed kitten, but it kept those shoes in service for a long stretch.

There came a day when a fellow was in high school and of an age, because he earned his own spending money, to take care of the mending of his shoes himself. He experimented with the luxury of his first rubber heels. It was like walking on air, he felt, and he promised himself he never would have any but rubber heels as long as he lived. The days of the steel clamps were gone forever. It was as if he had cast aside his shackles.

That Summer, he bought—with his own money—his first pair of yellow low shoes with pointed toes!

Long Ones

The big day came, usually at about fifteen. Some, of course, luckier than the rest because they had reached man's height earlier, would strut out in long ones at the age of fourteen—or in some cases, even at thirteen. But the average, I should say, was about fifteen.

Of course, the young men of today, who are piled into their long pants when they're five and even younger, will never enjoy the thrill that blessed our generation. I am sorry for them!

Believe me, it was something to look forward to—the wonderful day when, once and for all, a fellow could kiss his knickers good-bye and present himself to the admiring world in trousers with cuffs, that embraced the top of his shoes, or if he wore low kicks, nestled just high enough to permit his socks to show.

And don't ignore those socks.

Some with old mossbacks for parents had to wait, perhaps, another year before they were allowed to dispense with those long, black, ribbed stockings that were always turning bottle-green after the second or third washing.

Fortunately, my father was a tolerant, understanding gentleman and the Saturday evening we traveled downtown to Bank Street to pick out my first man's suit, he remarked quite casually that we were going to stop over later at the men's wear department to select a few pairs of socks and—well, I shiver with excitement even as I write this— my first men's-style garters to replace those sissy affairs which looped around the stockings above the knees!

The difference between buying a kid suit with knickers and a man's outfit with long trousers was made apparent right away. First there was considerable fuss by the polite, smiling salesman. He made quite a ceremony of telling you to stand in front of an arrangement of mirrors which showed the back of your shoulders and the side view if you posed at the proper angle. Then, while you watched through the wonderful mirrors, he pulled out one of those self-winding tape measures and began spreading the ribbon from shoulder to shoulder across the back.

"H'm," he murmured, "just as I thought. Yes—I think I've got it."

Then the tape went across the chest and around the waist and down the legs.

This was merely a delightful preliminary. The next step was the selection of the suit. The polite salesman took one after another from the racks, spread each out under the lights, tugged at the fabric, rubbed a hand over it this way and that, keeping up a running stream of informative chatter concerning the wearing qualities.

I was all for picking the very first one shown, but my more conservative and experienced father insisted upon taking time before reaching the ultimate decision. We finally decided upon something in blue serge. It had three buttons in front and a vest which buttoned so high that there was scarcely any "V" left to reveal the shirt. The price of the suit was $11, which my father thought was rather a lot of money to spend. But this was not a place in which you could bargain and he made no attempt to, merely expressing his conviction, mildly, that it was expensive.

However, even as my heart was tumbling down into my shoes from despair, he said, "We'll take it if it fits."

"If it fits?" echoed the salesman in hurt tones. "Why you don't think for a minute we would let this fine young man walk out of our store with a suit which does not fit? We have a reputation to live up to, you know."

My father felt very sheepish and apologetic. I went into a little cubicle and put on my suit.

My first long pants!

Then to my dismay I discovered something. There were no cuffs! As I looked up at the salesman in bitter disappointment, he must have sensed what was in my mind, for he hastened to assure me he was going to take another measurement with the tape for length and width of trousers—and then we would decide on the cuffs. Personally, he favored a two-inch cuff, although there were some who liked it 2½ inches. We compromised with 2¼ inches.

So I stepped out again in front of the mirror and was measured. The obliging salesman said the alterations would be made Monday, and if we came in for it Tuesday, he was certain the suit would be ready. Did my father want to pay in full now—or leave a deposit? My cautious father said he would leave a deposit and pay the balance when we came in for the suit.

This was something of a disappointment, too. Three whole days to wait. How could I live through the long hours? But I hadn't forgotten my father's promise—socks —and men's garters.

We spent almost half an hour at the counter, but finally

the purchase was made. Three pairs—that was to be the start. Later, my father assured me, we would buy three more. They were not fancy hosiery, just plain black—no clocks, no elaborate ribs—just black cotton socks. But to me they were the last word. Price: three pairs for thirty-five cents! The garters took less time to select. I simply picked the first pair shown.

On Tuesday I walked out of the store with the suit in a cardboard box under my arm. That night I tried it on over the new socks and garters, with my father showing me how to adjust the supports. The following morning I wore my outfit to school.

It was a trying experience. I felt that every eye was upon me as I entered the classroom. There were hot stones on the back of my neck and torches searing my cheeks. The big, grown-up feeling had given way to one of tortured self-consciousness. Whispers near me were jeers, I knew. The giggles of the girls were in derision. I was miserable. Were the cuffs too large? Was I imagining my socks were falling? The vest felt altogether too tight.

It wasn't until I was on my way home that afternoon that it suddenly occurred to me. No one, not a single fellow or girl in my class, had said one word about the change in my status from knickers to long pants.

No one had even noticed!

Town Dudes

Clothes didn't make the man in our town.

Don't misunderstand me. People dressed with taste and the wealthier citizens wore fine tailor-made garments and spent hours selecting imported fabrics. It was rumored that Mr. Chase, head of the big manufacturing plant, paid as much as $100 for a suit. We had several fashionable dressmakers for the women, but most of our female population found their needs adequately answered in the stores downtown.

I recall vaguely that one of the two dudes of the neighborhood was regarded with scorn by our elders. I know my mother used to grow hysterical if he came by when she was sitting on the porch and she had one of us younger ones or a neighbor as an audience for her remarks.

"You think maybe he wears ruffles under those pants?" she would ask. "I think I'll give him a bottle of cologne water. With that shirt he should have something. It should smell sweet, like he is. Isn't he sweet?" And she would giggle and rock her chair.

Poor fellow, he was probably harmless enough. We called him "Pidge," for no good reason that I can remember. If ever a man was a fashion plate, it was he. Long before they began displaying them in the store windows, he would have the shoes with the narrowest points, the suit with the tightest pinch-back jacket, the snappiest turn-up brim on his hat. The buttons on his shoes weren't just plain black or brown; they were mother-of-pearl. Once my father had to slap my mother on the back and tell her not to act so hysterically. "Pidge" had passed by with his high shoes buttoned by what seemed to be rubies.

You must not think he was one of those effeminate men. Indeed, he was quite the one for the ladies, and at the dances in Buckingham Hall, he was the lad who executed the fanciest and fastest two-step or the waltz. I'll never forget how impressed I was, after having completed my course at Prof. Ricks' Dancing School, when I watched "Pidge" do his version of the waltz at a public affair. It was practically all reverse and you may rely on it that he had a most elaborate silk handkerchief which he kept against his partner's back, so his hand wouldn't touch her dress and soil it.

As far as I know, "Pidge" was an agreeable chap, and I don't recollect that I ever saw him sulk or act rudely. But the fact was evident that he was not a man's man. Most of the time, except at dances, he was alone, and when he did have a companion it was a girl.

The other dude was a middle-aged man named Thompson, who apparently had an independent income, for no one ever recalled that he had worked at any time. He lived with two elderly aunts, both widows. Like "Pidge," he was usually alone. Occasionally, he would be seen walking down Cooke Street between his two aunts. At such times, none of the three seemed to be interested in one another. There was no conversation, and usually they looked straight ahead as they walked.

Mr. Thompson also dressed in what we considered the extreme of fashion and I take it for granted that his clothes and his shoes and his hats were the most expensive to be obtained. In fact, the report was that every so often he went to New York to do his buying.

People made fun of "Pidge" but never of Mr. Thompson. They were both dudes, but my mother never seemed to find anything comical to say about dudish Mr. Thompson. But let poor amiable "Pidge" pass by, and she would let loose.

When I went back to the home town many years later for a visit—I was then a brand-new Broadway columnist—I saw "Pidge" in Exchange Place. The fifteen years since I had last seen him had left their mark. He was an old man. But he was still the dude and sported a cane, something that required considerable courage in my neighborhood. I stopped to say hello and introduced myself, but he merely gave me a vague look, smiled uncertainly and moved on.

I learned he had wed a nice widow woman about his own age, and the two apparently were getting along contentedly on her income. My inquiry about Mr. Thompson drew the information that he had died of a heart attack while at the movies. One of my former newspaper buddies still working on the fine old hometown newspaper that had given me my start told me that when they undressed Mr. Thompson for the medical examiner, they discovered that both his undershirt and shorts were monogrammed.

"There was nothing phony about him," commented my friend. "He was a thorough dude."

About a Boat

We always wore our best clothes when Pa and Ma took us for an occasional excursion to New York on the old *Richard Peck*. And come to think of it, it was on one of these trips that I ran into "Pidge" sitting on deck next to a young woman. He was holding one of her hands tightly and whispering insistently. Finally, I saw him reach over and put his arms around her and kiss her. Immediately, I rushed back into the cabin to tell Mama. She merely grunted and said, "Like two women kissing. Like tea without sugar."

What a glorious vessel the *Richard Peck* was! Such thick carpets! Such polished rails! Those soft, cushiony chairs! You went out on deck and sat in a collapsible canvas seat and the water sprayed up over the rails and smelled clean and salty and adventurous. That was it. There was adventure every time you sailed on the good ship *Richard Peck*.

The thrill never dwindled. First of all, there was that wonderful port to which we were sailing, the Magic City of the East—New York.

In those early days of the great trips on the magnificent *Richard Peck* another thrill awaiting one passenger at least was the ride on the cars pulled by horses. They still had horse cars then, and it was a wonderful adventure to ride in them. Usually my father would take me to a lunchroom down near the Battery, where we had magnificent crullers which cost a penny apiece and a big glass of milk which cost two cents.

In later years, there was even more fun taking that trip from New Haven to New York on the *Peck*. At seventeen, a fellow never thought of wasting his time by traveling on a stuffy train. The boat trip usually took eight to ten hours. There were always sure to be some mighty nice girls aboard to flirt with. If you were lucky—and the type—some fine friendships resulted. In my case, it was usually a matter of wistful watching, while the other boys who had dash and knew how to wear clothes went right up to the pretty girls boldly and started discussing brazen subjects like the speed the boat was making and some of the new jazz songs.

I recall, too, that most of us brought along our lunch and supper wrapped in waxed paper, but once an uncle of mine, who was a bachelor, treated me to a meal on the boat. I must say I never tasted anything more delicious in all my life.

My last trip on the *Richard Peck* was made shortly after I came out of the Army in the First World War and had just been married. I took my bride on the trip—as a substitute for a honeymoon on bigger boats to places farther off in other countries. My wife and I agree it was the most wonderful sea voyage we have ever enjoyed.

I don't remember where the *Richard Peck* docked in New York but I have an idea it was not far from a point up the street where I am writing this chapter.

Rain on South Street

Some devilish impulse inspired the very energetic gentleman who arranges office locations in the building where I labor daily to set my desk in a room with two large windows, each urging the susceptible eye to a feast of Manhattan's most ghostlike thoroughfare, the street known as South.

So often when my duty has been to record the vagaries of the throbbing metropolis, the words registered by the battered instrument on which these anemic fingers play daily have formed expressions of wonder or sympathy with the mood of a river-front thoroughfare.

Outside on South Street, there is rain, and no rain can compare with a downpour on this river lane. South Street is a street of moods, and none of them is happy. South Street is gray and somber at dawn, cold and repelling and brutally aloof at twilight, sad and deserted and mysterious at midnight.

The waters of the river sob as they beat against the docks and wall. At night passing freighters and steamers whine out their warning signals. The three bridge skeletons arch gruesomely across the stream. Trucks, large and small, thunder back and forth throughout the day, but at night and on Sundays, only an occasional automobile speeds on as if to get away from the street and its sinister spell.

The shops along South Street smack of musty mystery. Maritime supplies, anchors and ropes, equipment for fishing smacks. Lunch-carts, warehouses, fish stalls. Always there is the odor of dead fish, and in the cold bleakness of the rain-swept street, a sight that stabs the heart. Men of such wretchedness as to chill the marrow huddle about their improvised stove: a garbage can giving out a flame that warms meagerly. Unshaven, dirty men of all ages gather around this garbage can, seeking warmth while the rain drenches their rags and chokes their fire.

Often a little group huddles near the river wall. Not all are vagrants, for there is a blue-coat of authority here and there and a white-coat of the hospital crew. A body, dripping wet, is dragged out. Some forlorn hopeless wanderer, despairing of life, has sought the soothing oblivion of the river.

On a rainy Sunday afternoon, the barges linger in dock with no sign of life aboard, although down below, the families who make these barges their Winter and Summer homes are congregated. You wonder how they endure the monotony and dreariness of it. There is no excitement or glamor aboard the barge, for the women I see on them are usually old before their time, exhaustion marked in their lined faces, weariness in their eyes.

So the rain falls on South Street and the wind screams derisively. At twilight the building across the river will light up and the waters will reach out and daub themselves with its reflection. But South Street will remain sinister. It can only induce melancholy reflections.

CHAPTER SEVEN

Crime

Our town was predominantly Irish-American although it boasted hundreds of citizens of Yankee stock whose forebears had fought in the Colonial and Revolutionary Wars. There was also a goodly percentage of Lithuanians who had settled in the southern section of the city, a district we know as Brooklyn. In addition, there were quite a few Italians and Jews and a scattering of hard-working Negroes. But the Irish ran our town, and ran it well.

There was no unusual crime problem. Occasionally, there were Saturday-night brawls and, of course, the police blotter had its daily quota of drunks and vagrants, but the city court cases were none too exciting. Once in a while—actually, only twice that I can recall—Martin Dalton's establishment was raided and the painted Jezebels brought to the station house in the Black Maria. Sometimes there was a little cutting-up at a house party in the Brooklyn section when the wine had flowed too freely and once there was quite a free-for-all when the late Carlo Tresca came to town to address an open-air meeting.

Otherwise, the days and the nights were uneventful

and the citizens went about their labors serenely. However, there would come a rare day when the town would pick up its daily paper and learn to its delighted horror that there had been a murder, real, honest-to-goodness fatal shooting or slicing, with promise of more sensational details to come in subsequent inquiries and court developments.

There was the time, for instance, when Sophie Kritchman and her new boy friend decided that Sophie's old boy friend was superfluous. They set upon him with sharp knives and rocks, crushing his skull and slashing his throat from ear to ear. But the fellow was tough and lingered for a day or two in the bushes where he had been dragged, sipping dew from the grass in a desperate but futile effort to keep alive.

The details are vague in my mind, but I know he was completely and irretrievably dead when they found his body—and Sophie and her fellow conspirator found themselves in a bad way with the law.

Somehow, they escaped capital punishment, but were sentenced to life imprisonment. A few years ago Sophie was finally released on the grounds of ill health!

Then there was the stoutish but evidently desirable Bessie Wakefield who developed a passion for John Plew, a chap with vague antecedents. Bessie was unwilling to carry on with Plew while her innocent and inoffensive husband was still alive. She solved the delicate situation by killing him, with Plew's aid.

The murder took place near Cheshire and was similar in detail to the disposal of Sophie Kritchman's man; that is to say, knives and rocks were used. Plew was hanged by the neck at Wethersfield, but the soft-hearted Governor commuted Bessie's sentence from a neck-stretch to a life stretch in the jug. A couple of years ago, I read that Bessie, too, had been pardoned.

There was another act of fatal mayhem committed by a John Rikteraitis on his wife, but John was a male and they hanged him without sympathy and, of course, without considering commutation of sentence. It might have been different if he had been Joanna, for ours was a chivalrous state in those days.

There may have been one or two other murders in our town during the days when I was young, but, on the whole, a citizen could walk the streets at any hour of the night without fear, and some of the older citizens never thought of turning the key in the lock when they retired for the evening.

The thievery was of the petty variety, and the occasional burglaries were minor, too. There was one period when a series of holdups took place in the North End section, but a couple of extra cops were added and the crime wave subsided.

All in all, the youngsters in our middle-class neighborhood had little contact with the shoddier phases of life. Occasionally we read or heard the details of a lurid murder elsewhere which made our few thrilling episodes seem tame in comparison with a lynching down South or a sensational hold-up out West.

But on the whole, we concerned ourselves mainly with problems which revolved around tyrannical, intolerant school teachers, misunderstanding, tight-wad parents, Yale football heroes, the latest Dick Merriwell, an exchange of a Horatio Alger, Jr., the Sunday funnies and an occasional visit to the movie houses.

As a fellow approached the adulthood of eleven or twelve, he became vaguely aware that there were women about whom it was polite merely to whisper. They were "bad" women who would be much better off dead. There were wicked men, too, but just what their vices were was beyond the ken of the twelve-year-olds in our neighborhood.

Our newspapers were reluctant about mentioning anything that couldn't be discussed over the breakfast or dinner table with the children present. I can't remember ever seeing such horrifying words as "rape," "dope-addict," "prostitute" or the like in print, until one morning, a bolder, brazen "scandal" sheet was passed around in school.

One day, I was out with a much older chap—a man of seventeen—who worked in a drug store after high school. We were walking down North Main Street, when out of a doorway stepped a thin, pasty-faced fellow.

"Hey, son, gotta butt?" he asked, in a thin, whining voice. My friend proffered his package of Sweet Caps and the ragged chap took one and sucked on it hungrily while my buddy lit it.

Then the precocious seventeen-year-old drug clerk said something that mystified me, but immediately made him a man of the world in my eyes.

"On the stuff, ain'tcha?" he snapped, actually in the form of an accusation.

"Yeah," whispered the man. "You, too?" he asked eagerly.

"Nope," replied my friend. "But," he added, proudly, "I can tell. I'm wise to ya. I work in a drug store. Nothin' I don't know about it."

There ensued a colloquy which was Greek to me, but from which I gathered that if my pal, the drug clerk, only would get him "some," there was nothing the stranger wouldn't do for him. Just give him his address and as soon as he got into some dough he would send it all.

My buddy shook his head. No, that was out. The stranger ought to know better than to ask him.

The little thin man whined and wheedled and pleaded, and his eyes were those of a man in despair.

"Be a good fellow. Just this once," he urged.

Finally the drug clerk said okay. He would go over to the store and see if he could sneak "some." The fellow was to wait right there. It would take fifteen to twenty minutes, maybe longer.

"You're sure coming back, now. You mean it, don'cha?" pleaded the stranger.

"I wouldn't say so if I wasn't going to try," my friend reassured him.

I went along with him and on the way he explained condescendingly that the man was a "dope fiend." Also, he said, he took it with a needle. There were some who breathed a white powder like snuff, but it was more powerful with a needle.

I wasn't horrified. I wasn't indignant that my friend should be willing to help out an addict. It was all so new to me that my only reaction was one of curiosity. When we arrived at the drug store my friend ran in and came out again in less than five minutes.

There was disappointment in his face.

"Shucks," he mumbled. "Can't get near it. Old Barney's in there and there ain't no chance. Shucks, that poor guy, I can't go back and tell him."

So we didn't get back and I don't know what the "poor guy" did or thought or whatever happened to him, but shortly after I took out a copy of De Quincey's *Confessions of an Opium Eater* from the Public Library, not without having to explain to the library clerk, who questioned me for taking the grown-up's book out on a school-boy's card, that it was for my mother who had mislaid hers.

I took it home, eager to read about this forbidden practice, but after a half dozen pages I found myself bored and yawning. I didn't return to De Quincey until many, many years later.

For weeks I was the life of the party as I told the boys and the girls about the "dope fiend" who had popped out of a North Main Street doorway. With each telling the story grew more and more dramatic until I am certain that, to this day, those of my neighborhood pals who are still alive think of him, if they do at all, as a desperate character, an escaped murderer, a villain of the deepest dye, whom Sobol, bravely and defiantly, sent packing on his way.

Characters

There were a few odd birds in our neighborhood who invited the scorn and derision of us younger ones, but never the pity that perhaps the more tolerant adults might have shown. We had no one who might be described as the town drunk, chiefly because ours was a sizeable community and there never was just one hooch-hoister to pick on. There were dozens. The characters were fewer and they stood out from the normal citizenry.

There was a middle-aged fellow with a wisp of a mustache, not unlike the late Herr Hitler's, who barked like a dog. As he walked down the street, his head would twist from left to right every few seconds, then it would jerk spasmodically upward as he emitted four or five staccato barks and then a long long piercing whine like a hound in distress.

No one seemed to know much about him, and none of

the elders was sympathetic enough to caution the youngsters not to jeer. We called him, Willie the Dog Man, and, I suspect, made his life miserable.

Of course, the stories they told about him were many and fantastic. We were asked to believe that he was an orphan, who as a baby had been chained by an unfeeling guardian to several irritable mongrels. At first they snarled at him and bit him and abused him until he had learned to snarl and bite back.

Another story was that his mother, shortly before his birth, had been attacked by a mad airedale which had sunk its fangs into her neck and that, even while she was still hovering between life and death, the infant had come into the world whining like a puppy.

These were only two of many explanations, but, actually, no one knew anything about Willie—not even his real name, where he worked, if he worked, or how he managed to live from day to day.

There was no evidence that he had a single friend in all the world to worry over him. Always a lone figure, he would shuffle down the street, barking and wailing while little boys followed, hooting at him.

The Duchess was not quite so forlorn a character. The Duchess was a slim, middle-aged chap who wore a corset, frilly shirts and walked down the avenue with quick, mincing steps on high-heeled shoes. His face was heavily rouged, his eyelashes beaded, his eyelids a purple smear, his small mouth a crimson cupid's bow.

On several occasions, he was picked up by the police, but there never was any evidence against him, nor any specific charges. Naturally we called him a "fairy," although some of us were still vague about just what the word meant.

In spite of suspicions, and the Duchess' obvious preference for feminine adornments, I must repeat, no one could actually point a finger at him. He was an Alsatian, and like Willie the Dog Man, apparently had no friends. At least, whenever we saw him he was alone.

He must have had courage. The kids jeered and exploded rasping noises between their lips at him, and the older toughies who loitered around Exchange Place were even more vicious. In addition to their obscene taunts, they jostled him and manhandled him whenever he passed by until the cop came along and prodded him contemptuously with his night stick, usually shoving the club into the "fairy's" back harder than usual.

Now that I think of it, he never flinched or fled from his molesters. Some of the more tolerant folks considered him merely a harmless crackpot, and really felt sorry for him.

There came a time when the Duchess was no longer seen in the streets of our town. One day there appeared a story in a Bridgeport paper that a man's fully-clothed body had floated ashore at Savin Rock outside of New Haven.

Only it wasn't a man at all—but a woman! One of the reporters recognized her. It was the Duchess.

Then there was the wealthy Lon Horgan, the wholesale butcher, who became more and more pompous as his moneybags swelled. An eccentric fellow, he somehow reminded you of the legend of Canute who ordered the waves to subside. Horgan walked along the streets and stopped people with a flourish of his hand so that he could pass. Folks did halt because most of them were impressed by his importance. Then he took to stopping automobiles whenever he wanted to cross the street. In the tangled business traffic, he would start across, waving his hands in a peremptory command for autos to halt. They would, too, and he continued to his destination.

One day he held out his arm in front of an out-of-town auto. The auto did not stop. It struck Lon Horgan and killed him.

Crazy Sadie was a harmless loon who liked to sing. In appearance, she was not unlike that pitiful waif, widely publicized by New York columnists as Broadway Rose, but Crazy Sadie was no pursuer of celebrities nor was she ever known to have solicited coins. She was really a sight. Her shoes were run-down, high-buttoned affairs over which she wore frayed spats. Around her neck, Winter or Summer, there was always a ragged red scarf. She wore her hair in curls tied in ribbons, each of the five or six curls in a band of different color. She affected a party-white make-up, except for her lips which looked like a raw wound.

Crazy Sadie would join any group of more than two, uninvited, and start singing. I can't recall the songs she sang were ever anything anyone had sung before. They were neither popular songs nor good old standbys, neither hymns nor the familiar folk classics. But there were words and there were tunes. I think, perhaps, long before any of us knew what they were, Crazy Sadie was chanting calypsos of her own creation.

One day one of our prominent citizens died and almost everyone of importance in the State came to the church for the funeral. As they carried the casket out, there was Crazy Sadie yowling her repertoire, incorporating into each song a great deal about the distinguished late citizen's background and sins. They arrested Sadie for disturbing the peace, but she was released the following morning, and the word was whispered around that nothing short of arson or murder would bring Sadie into the clutches of the cops again.

In those days, the lockup was downstairs under the police station, and Sadie sang her songs all night—but loud. It not only annoyed the fellow-lodgers, but, what was worse, the station attendants couldn't keep their minds on their poker game.

Gals in Tights

One day posters appeared all over town, announcing that burlesque was coming into the Jacques Theatre. This caused plenty of excitement in high-school circles but none elsewhere and I certainly cannot recall that any hue or cry was raised by the church folk.

I had never seen burlesque in the flesh, but I knew it was something delightfully sinful because I had seen pictures in the *Police Gazette* whenever I went to the barber shop for my monthly haircutting.

Burlesque meant voluptuous Jezebels, full-bosomed, shapely limbed, flirtatious and dangerous. Just looking at one from a distance was excitingly dangerous. Perhaps, to be able to speak to one, to shake hands with her even, well, this was too much even for the blood pressure of a healthy, if immature youth.

Strangely enough, though this was the first burlesque show I had ever attended, I can recall neither the title nor any of the principals. I sat in my balcony seat, thrilled beyond words as the wonderful, beautiful, glorious, heavenly ladies of the burlesque ensemble came out, sometimes in their white tights, sometimes in their pink tights, sometimes in voluminous diaphanous dresses, sometimes in abbreviated skirts. There was no strip tease, and if the patter of the comedians was smutty or double-entendre, I must confess I just didn't catch on.

I do recall, though, that no group of sirens ever looked

more glamorous than these shoddy, none too youthful, fat and thin and very tired girls of the burlesque. It was a cheap troupe and an underpaid one, but, of course, I knew none of this at the time.

Then, some years later, a colorful character of the show world came in from New York, took over the Jacques which had been closed for several seasons, and brought back burlesque. His name was Jim "Apple Sauce" Clancy, a lovable, voluble, energetic individual who had worked for the theatrical potentate, Sylvester Z. Poli, quarreled with him and had come into Waterbury to embark upon his own venture.

He acquired the "Apple Sauce" because that was his favorite expression. As far as I know, he may have originated the phrase to mean what we still take it to mean when we use it by way of mild opprobrium. Another favorite term of scorn used by Jim was "Aw, that's humpty-dumpty Logan."

At any rate, Clancy was one who believed in doing things right. Having decided that the town was hungry for top-flight burlesque, he imported none but the best, at that time operated by the Columbia wheel. So it was that I first came to view on the stage such comic or otherwise talented gentlemen as James Barton, Lester Allen, Bert Lahr, Dave Marion (Snuffy, the Cabman), Sliding Billy Watson, Beef Trust Watson, Jean Bedini, Harry K. Morton—many others.

The girls were beautiful, the gags simply too hilarious for words, if slightly outrageous, and the comedians the funniest men in the world. Invariably there was the olio. Someone who might be slim and young or stoutish and elderly and wearing a "dome doily" would come out and sing "When Irish Eyes are Smiling" or "Mother Machree." The house, which had been roaring at the bawdy gags or lewdly ogling the undraped beauties, would now burst into tumultuous applause and sometimes the women in the audience would cry.

Occasionally, one of the older lads, bolder than the rest, would "date" a sumptuous queen of the burleycue and parade her proudly at midnight over to George Mulligan's or to the snootier Hodson's. These dates, though, were rare, because Jim Clancy had some sort of understanding with the manager of the visiting troupe that the girls would not mingle with the townsfolk. He wanted no civic body to start a crusade, and I can't recall that, during the Clancy reign, there was any suspicion of a campaign to rid the town of the evil influence of burlesque.

Of course, this rowdier sister of show business had advanced since those first obscure productions that had excited our town. The girls now seemed younger, happier and better dressed, both on and off stage. The comedians actually were funny, and many of them went on to the higher strata of the theatre and into the movies and radio. I repeat, there was no strip tease and no particular nudity. The wicked moments of the show usually came when a curvaceous doll strutted out and then plunged into a torrid cooch.

As the years passed, Jim Clancy became a solid citizen of the community. Whenever there was a municipal drive for funds, he was usually on the active committee. The town mourned his death and the local papers ran his lengthy obituary on Page One. His funeral was one of the most largely attended in many years.

Not a little of Jim Clancy's success—and that of his burlesque enterprise—was due to a shy but witty fellow who could write a mighty readable streak of wordage. He was on one of the local newspapers, and Jim, who had read his by-lined sports stories, invited him to become his publicity man on the side. There was nothing unethical about this in those days. The young newspaper fellow was quite happy to earn that extra money to fatten out the thinnish pay envelope. His name was Dan Parker and he is now the famed New York sports columnist.

There are countless anecdotes in connection with Jacques Theatre, before and after Clancy's regime. One which became more or less a legend concerns an episode which took place just about the time I must have been kicking off my swaddling clothes. The show at the Jacques was a comic opera and the two comedians were Messrs. Wolff and Woolley, abetted by a tall, strikingly attractive girl with a beautiful figure and a shock of red hair. The high-brow drama critic for the afternoon paper, reviewing the production, lashed into the girl for her rowdy horseplay on stage. She invited him to return and see the show the next night. She would so much like him to view her as she really was.

What followed then was a shambles. The beautiful amazon went through her routine with the zest and fury of a dozen stage demons. She pretended she was a pitcher at a ball game; she picked up Wolff and Woolley and pitched them into the audience. She did a split. She turned cart wheels. She ran up the side of the first entrance and dived back on the stage in a belly-slide. She drove the orchestra out of the pit, chased the company into the flies, wrestled Wolff and Woolley in a sequence of ground and lofty tumbling which left them all but stripped to the buff and made her final exit with both limp comedians draped about her body as she stalked off with a blood-curdling yell at the cringing critic down in the second row.

That girl's name was Marie Dressler.

Spring Fancy
—and Fact

Spring tapped the Old Man lightly on the shoulder and urged: "Go home, Pop, you're tired." Old Man Winter gave her an icy stare, mumbled "You're a fresh kid" and staggered away. Spring shivered, clutched my arm and we walked up Swing Lane.

New York's poignant dusk was upon us and the huge globe of neon sinking down at street's end blinded us. "I never knew," murmured Spring, "the sun could knife a person's eyes so on 52d street."

Gray-haired cameo-profiled George Jean Nathan and a fragile slip of an Oriental girl were entering Twenty-One. We nodded to Jack Kriendler as he directed the face-washing of the jockey-statues.

A few doors away, thinnish Eddie Davis was surveying the installation of a lady in several striking and altogether unconventional poses. One gathered she was a minor apostle of the strip-tease.

Charlie, the cabman philosopher, greeted us from his stand in front of Tony's. "Haven't had two decent loads today," he groaned. Dizzy Dan, elderly eccentric, passed. Utterly wise man or perfect loon, he never wears a coat or hat; his shirt is always open at the neck; his pants cut at the knees, exposing the bare legs. His close and inevitable pal is a tiny, hairy and weary-looking dog.

We were at Seventh Avenue, a paper clip's toss from Broadway. Now the mellow purple dusk had surrendered to the chromatic dazzle that is Broadway's night. The city's millions were pushing toward early dinners, to cinema huts, to hotel-lobby trysts. The loud but pleasant noises of the Thrilling Thoroughfare crowded in upon us. The peculiar

121

undefinable odor which is distinctive of Broadway enveloped us. It was exciting.

At 50th and Broadway, out of the tangled mob, a sinister face melted into a scowl of recognition. I saluted and shouted, "Hi, Pete."

I thought: "What a magnificent face! As if it had torn itself from an illustration for a gangster story. The scar, the tight little eyes, the thin, shut lips."

I knew better. He was a soft-spoken, gentle soul, an amateur connoisseur of art. There was no finer collection in all Manhattan than his prized assortment of etchings and paintings of past and present masters.

We walked another block, and now Spring was merely a lovely girl, slightly chilled, hinting that perhaps a cab would be welcome. The dumpy, white-haired little gardenia woman was at my elbow. She thrust a corsage upon my companion, at the same time directing the full beam of her sales personality upon me.

"I guarantee," she persisted, "on a lady like that they won't fade."

The lady who was no longer Spring concluded I was an old man and left me for a warm cab. I had no appetite, and the newsreel theatre offered an hour's diversion.

Standing in front of me at the ticket kiosk was a short middle-aged fellow with unruly hair dripping down from under a felt fedora, sizes too small for the leonine head. As the cashier pushed the oblong stub toward him, he turned for a second and I thought I recognized him. I wasn't sure, but it seemed to me he might be Lion Feuchtwanger. I was too timid to inquire.

I walked into the lobby. Coming toward me was the ubiquitous, petiferous zany known as Broadway Rose, the loon who used to follow a Name for blocks undismayed, undeterred, unoffended by rebuffs. The authorities finally put her away.

Tonight she wore a wafer-like top-piece from which, out of what appeared to be a slightly mutilated head of lettuce, popped three large cherries, looking like the pawnbroker's symbol dipped in ketchup. Her high-buttoned shoes made due obeisance to Fashion. The toes were cut away (with a razor, no doubt). Her dress was something in yellow which flirted with the ankles in front but skirted only the knees in back.

There was cordial good-fellowship in the eyes of Broadway Rose as she hailed me. "Gee, you going in?" she inquired in her habitual sing-song. It was not so much a query as an indication of pity that I should waste my time.

"Hah, they told me Frankie was in there. So I spend good money. And who you think is in there? Frankie? Nah! Truman is in there. Ha, ha, ha! Truman is in there. Yeh, in the pickshures. Say, you ain't gimme a quarter in God knows how long. How about it, you gonna gimme a quarter, yeh?"

I eluded Broadway Rose's none-too-gentle but obviously solicitous clutch at my nearer elbow. The man who I thought might be Feuchtwanger had already entered the darkness of the theatre. Now I was settled in a seat in back.

Broadway Rose was right; there was no Frank Sinatra here tonight, but she lied to me about Truman. The hour of pictures skipped across the screen without a single shot of Truman. I didn't care much.

I was restless. I walked over to the Stork Club and entered the windowless, lopsided oval known as the Cub Room. There is a soothing unobtrusiveness of light above and over the Cub Room, and even before the first drink, a feeling that everything is pinkish, blending into a vague orange.

Fret and rush, impatience and melancholy, anger, sorrow and pain slip off like the seven veils of Salomé.

Across the room sat the most beautiful model in the

world. *If you asked them, quickly, artists like Dean Cornwell and Arthur William Brown, Bradshaw Crandell and James Montgomery Flagg would say: "Of course, she is. Show me anyone more beautiful."*

Her exquisite features have inspired many a young and old susceptible to save magazine covers. She has been the radiant queen dominating hosiery and hat advertisements, cigarette posters, soap and lotion spreads.

A lovely person, well-bred, nicely educated, eagerly accepted in both Broadway and Park Avenue circles—surely the highest type of American beauty.

I thought: "Isn't it a pity this gorgeous orchid has had only colorless romances? I thought I could find a dozen, three dozen, five hundred drab, little stenographers wooed by obscure clerks who had a gayer time of it.

At a corner table sat a handsome youth who in other and fancier days would have been labeled "matinee idol." A tall fellow with somnolent dark eyes. From the rush of silken black hair, a rebellious lock had torn loose from its leash of grease to come pawing over forehead and eyes. He slumped there with half droopy eyelids and the blondish wide-eyed girl at his side kept gazing at him out of swooning eyes. He seemed quite content to be wooed openly by the baby debutante.

Sherman Billingsley came over. "Nice people here tonight," he murmured. I said yes, there were some nice people around tonight. I caught Jack Spooner's eye. Jack is the gray-haired, distinguished-looking captain of waiters in the Cub. In his day he had known and served such dignitaries of past headlines and feature pages as Diamond Jim Brady, Harry K. Thaw, Evelyn Nesbit, Lillian Russell, Otto Kahn, David Belasco, and the late Theodore Roosevelt.

Jack came over. A deck of cards popped out of a sleeve. He fanned them into a spread. He passed a hand over them.

All hearts. He passed a hand over them again—all spades.
Jack began to unload his little cargo of card tricks, and the
beautiful model joined us and sat down with us and held
my hand. It didn't mean anything because we're old friends
and she likes my wife very much.

I was restless again.

I moved on to the Copacabana and settled down at a table
near a post just as Mr. Joe Everglades Lewis was earnestly
describing his experience with an indifferent hotel clerk. He
said, "I told him 'I am not going to stand here and have you
tolerate me.' Well, he knew I had him! Anyone who takes
me for a damn fool makes no mistake."

The fat man at the ringside, named Shor, roared. A skinny,
wan-looking boy with a collossal bow tie chuckled. Bobby-
sockers swooned at the sight of him. He was their "Frankie."
The table to the left of us maintained its stone-chilled aloof-
ness. The boy was young and good-looking, the girl was
pretty, the woman middle-aged, slightly patrician—perhaps
the mother of either one of them or of both. They looked
as alike as three airmail stamps.

Mr. Lewis, wanted to sing. The hit song of 1943, he
droned was "Lili Marlene." He did not know that song, but
he would like to sing "Lily Farfel." This was a number he
did in his last picture—and "It was my last picture."

Mr. Eddy Duchin guffawed like mad. Mr. Ted Husing
yelled, "Oh, no! No!"

The boy, the girl and the middle-aged woman stared at
Joe, bored, resentful.

Mr. Lewis coughed. He pounded his chest. He looked up
at what might have been a heaven stitched with stars, but
was merely a slightly soiled low ceiling.

He coughed again, consumptively, and wrapped the collar
of his brown suitcoat tightly around his neck.

"I must get a room tonight," he said plaintively.

The tight-packed room roared its appreciation. Mr. Lewis pirouetted, shuffled, stepped gaily into a Joe Frisco tap dance.

There were some light notes from the piano and suddenly Mr. Austin Mack, his accompanist, loosened a melody, and Mr. Lewis began to sing.

"Please Mister Truman, be human, play the piano for me."

He looked back wickedly over his shoulder at Mr. Austin Mack. "You and your union—be careful, Mr. Mack, be careful. There's a man plays pretty good—prr-e-ettty good —in the White House."

There were titters and giggles. "Gee, that's good," whispered someone sitting to the right of Mr. H. V. Kaltenborn. "That Lewis always comes up with something new and good."

Mr. Lewis caroled bravely through to the finish on his one faltering note. I was still thinking of his chantey, the "H. V. Kaltenborn Blues" in which he sighs, "How thrillable, each syllable," and then I stared over at the intolerant threesome, the boy, the girl and the woman, hoping for a flicker of interest, just the slightest upbend of the lips, even a frown would have been acceptable.

They were like three wax dummies in a store window without the coloring, and not as well dressed. I thought of ice-cubes, the frozen north, the blizzard of '88 and my wife's expression the morning I came home lit up like a Douglas Leigh special, and began pounding the wall in a rhythmic beat because I felt like the drummer boy of Shiloh.

The drunk at the second table, right, was at it again. "Ahhh, nuts!" he shrieked. "Ahhhh, nuts!" Mr. Lewis opened his own jaws wide in a simulated guffaw. He closed his jaws. He tripped over swishily to the drunk. "Last time," he sang out, "I saw a mouth like yours, there was a hook in it! Hey, garsong, some sea-water for a carp, and don't spare the ickemay."

There was ice at the table with the threesome. They stared without sight. They listened without hearing. The boy sipped his drink. I said to myself, if Joe spots these three dead pans it'll break him up.

Joe was singing another song. "He never let failure go to his head" was the theme. The drunk at the second table, right, was being squelched by members of his own party and was acting up belligerently.

Now Mr. Lewis was humming and muttering, "Arrangements. Everything's arrangements. You gotta have arrangements."

"I'm suffering from a terrible handicap tonight," he said. "I have no talent."

Mr. Shor, the restaurateur, thought that was very funny. He pounded the back of the man to his left. He grinned over at Mr. Sinatra. "Sing the Groom Song, ya bum!" he roared over to Mr. Lewis.

Mr. Lewis was singing something else, though. It was a plaintive chant about a manicurist. Mr. Lewis was never completely happy, it seemed, unless the buffer was active across his shiny nails. Mr. Lewis was in ecstasy when he was being buffed by an expert manicurist.

There were signs of action at the table with the tiresome threesome. The girl yawned. The middle-aged woman who had been staring at the comedian as if he were some rare, outlandish exhibit released from the Smithsonian Institution, turned her back on him and faced the boy who was now displaying all the emotional reaction of a comatose herring.

Now Mr. Lewis was yielding to the insistent clamor of the paying customers. It was the saga of the bridegroom who was having trouble at his own wedding. I gathered from the song that, although the wedding hall was large enough

127

to hold a convention, there was no room for the groom. For some reason this pathetic situation threw the assembly at the Copacabana into convulsions.

But the frigid family of three rose stiffly and walked out, just as Mr. Lewis was explaining that Vincent Lopez and his gahdam piano got in—but "no room for the groom."

CHAPTER EIGHT

Love

The gang in my neighborhood avoided love involvements, but now and then one of us weakened and confessed that a certain girl truly was a "darb" or envied one of the other fellows his self-assurance, his almost cosmopolitan ease of manner in talking with a pretty girl. No shifting uneasily from foot to foot, no crimson flush, no looking from side to side, no fumbling with a jacket lapel or stammering or finding words choked off. How wonderful it was to be calm with a woman!

In those days a girl rarely ventured to telephone to a beau, asking him to meet her or take her to a dance. She would eat her heart out waiting patiently, and undoubtedly missed much thereby. On the other hand, there was a great thumping at the heart, a delicious spinal tingle for a chap of thirteen or fourteen when he telephoned and the sweet voice at the other end said, why, yes, she thought she would like very much to go to the freshmen get-together Friday night.

It was a grave social error to call up a girl at 5 o'clock Monday afternoon and expect her to go to the Palace or Jacques' with you that night. Her dignity was at stake.

Social protocol demanded that you contact her at least one or two days in advance. Many girls found themselves saying no, although they were dying to go to the dance, because the call came at the last minute. There was always the suspicion that perhaps someone else had been tried first and there had been a refusal.

Wild, flaming love seared me when I was a sophomore in high school and not too proficient in my studies. The object of my mad passion was a blondish beauty of Amazonian proportions who was a senior and a brazen flirt. She was being wooed by one of the men on the football squad.

There were ecstatic afternoons when, instead of translating his Anabasis or Caesar or whipping out a 200-word essay on Shakespeare, this thinnish, undersized loon would day-dream delirious visions in which he and the Amazonian senior starred in delightful boy-meets-girl situations with sugary endings which were just beginnings.

I made no plans to meet the desirable creature. It was not my idea to embark upon either an open or covert courtship. I sent no blazing love missives, indited no impassioned sonnets. It was sufficient that, occasionally in school assembly, I spotted her in the distance, that during a study period in the library she might be at the next table. I made no attempt on such occasions to address her nor to impress her with my presence.

My nights were troubled with prodding thoughts of her. My appetite wilted. I found little solace in the companionship of the neighborhood gang. When I wasn't in a mooning daze, I was irritable and snapped at my mother and talked back to my father.

I doubt whether my beloved one, my queen, my dream girl, ever knew I existed, but, though my heart bled in anguish when graduation took her out of school and out of my life, the day dreams remained to console and irritate me. Jagged-edged dirks ripped at me when wisps of rumors floated back that the beauteous and unattainable one was currently being courted by one of the tennis stars at Dartmouth, a doddering, old chap of twenty-one or thereabouts.

Assuagement of the fever came that summer when my interest swung over to another and younger woman of approximately fourteen. It may now be told that by the time the next term rolled around and I had been elevated to the dignity of a junior, the Amazonian senior was merely a pleasant memory.

Of all those neighborhood and school romances, only a half dozen or so bore more permanent fruit than passing infatuation. There was one fellow of our gang who began going with a little girl when he was twelve and she was scarcely ten. Of course, he was teased by us, but they clung to each other and in high-school days, when he was a senior and she was a sophomore, they were still inseparable.

I lost track of them and, indeed, since they were rather negative folks, gave very little thought to them until some months ago, when a hometown friend, meeting me at El Morocco one night, brought up the fellow's name. Eddie had developed tuberculosis, it seems, and while he was in a sanitarium, the girl's parents, by dint of nagging, had persuaded her to break off and marry a wealthy automobile distributor from a neighboring town.

For a time friends thought the fellow would die. He didn't want to live and kept calling for the girl all the time. But finally he responded to care, was released as cured and became a traveling salesman. Then, about eight years ago, he ran into the girl in Hartford, Conn. She had been married a long time, had two children, was matronly stout and looked her years.

"What a let down!" I exclaimed. "That finally put out the torch, didn't it?"

"You think!" retorted my Connecticut friend. "Do you know what Elsie did? She made her husband, a swell guy, too, with plenty of dough, give her a divorce. That's right. She gave him up and those two children—that was part of the agreement—and she married Eddie, Eddie, who didn't have a nickel—and spots on his lungs besides. She told him it was like she had never been married to that husband of hers at any time. With two children!"

Portrait of a Gentleman

More students enrolled for the Greek course in our school, I am willing to wager, than in any high school in the country. In fact, it was so strange that Principal Wilby personally began interviewing applicants. A classroom could hold only so many, and astute Principal Wilby suspected what the attraction was.

It was middle-aged, whimsical, gentle, jesting Jimmy Grafton. We called him Mister Grafton to his face, and he always seemed hurt when we did, but it was Jimmy behind his back. Of all the teachers from kindergarten up, Jimmy is the only one I cherish with the affection reserved for a close friend.

Professor Grafton was no fancy dresser. A confirmed bachelor, it was evident he had no one to chide him about his attire, to lay out the proper ensembles. His sartorial effects were incongruous, reaching something of a nadir when this lovable, absent-minded scholar appeared one day with a buttoned, high black shoe on one foot and a low laced shoe on the other.

He was an unorthodox teacher. His theory was that the best way to inculcate a love of the Greek language and ancient Greek thinking was to open up the class session with a discussion of the high cost of living, Christy Matthewson, the new lines of the Stutz Bearcat, Teddy Roosevelt or Jack Johnson.

Somehow, though, gradually we got around to Xenophon and the heroes of a magnificent by-gone era. I am willing to lay the long end of the odds that student for student, the Greek scholars turned out by Jimmy Grafton with his pleasant, painless methods of instruction, would stand comparison with any others in the country.

Jimmy was no dumbbell. He knew all the tricks and all the answers. Some among us who were the smart ones, we thought, used to plant our "pony" smack on the desk —not even hide it—and read from it brazenly when called upon to recite.

Once, when I was conducting my own personal "Don't Study Week," I read off the text boldly from the "pony" stuck into my *Anabasis*. Jimmy listened in that calm, sleepy, half-absent manner of his—usually he stared out of the windows—and when I had finished, he said, "Sobol, I think you ought to know. There are much better 'ponies' on the market. Remind me to bring you in the one they threw me out of class for using."

It was easy to start a discussion on any subject. Once a classmate asked Jimmy which was the correct plural— "fish" or "fishes." For five months, almost daily, the dispute raged, with arguments presented pro and con. The matter was never settled in my time, but the discussion saved many of us who had come in unprepared.

I had only one run-in with this fine old gentleman. In my senior year, I was working a full newspaper shift as a reporter, from two in the afternoon until midnight. (We had ten-hour newspaper days then, which meant anywhere from twelve to fourteen hours.) Naturally, I had very little sleep, since I was obliged to rise by seven each morning, in order to have time to wash, dress, eat breakfast and walk to school.

So it was that often I fell asleep in school. This occurred several times in Jimmy Grafton's class. The first time, from what I was given to understand later, he merely smiled and indicated I was to be permitted to slumber on. The second time he walked up the aisle and dropped a book on the desk, watched me awaken startled, grinned when he saw the sheepish look on my face and walked back to his platform.

The third time, however, he yelled, "Sobol, get out of this class. You're insulting."

I was suspended from Jimmy Grafton's class for the balance of the term. I felt pretty cheap and forlorn about it, but I was too ashamed to make overtures for a return to grace. Then one morning, about five days before graduation, Jimmy hailed me in the corridor.

"How about taking the exam?" he inquired.

"Gosh," I stammered, "I don't—well, I'm sure, Mr. Grafton, I can't pass now—not after all these months."

"Try them," urged Jimmy, and he walked on.

Talk about making up with your best girl! Well, that's nothing to the great inner glow I felt, now that Jimmy Grafton was speaking to me again.

I stayed away from my job that afternoon and boned up all through the day and the night. I wanted to make some sort of showing when I took the Greek exams the following morning.

It is my honest opinion to this day that I did not answer two of the twelve questions correctly. As a matter of fact, I was in pretty much of a mental fog from too much study the preceding day and from lack of sleep.

When the results were posted a few days later, opposite

my name was the mark of 86! And that was the mark Jimmy Grafton awarded me for the entire term. I still don't believe it.

As this is being written, Jimmy Grafton is still active, still wearing that shabby old brown derby—and still loved by everyone. God bless him!

Success with a Capital C

In my set, it was all right to plug on the high-school magazine and occasionally win a prize-essay contest or be on the committee for the annual school play, but no fellow could hope to win a popularity contest unless he made the basketball, football or baseball team. (I've listed them in the order of importance at good old Crosby.)

Classmates like Chic Durfee, Herm Huber, Aaron Berman, Mutt Davis, Bill Shea, Harry Liebeskind, Jim Nagle —they went out for everything, and some of them were like Frank and Dick Merriwell, heroes from the start. The way that Shea could belt a ball! Or run the pigskin through the massed opposition for a first down. Or that Durfee, when he grabbed the leather and popped it from dead center right through the hoop, with a few seconds left to play.

It wasn't only that the girls flocked around and made a fuss over them or that somehow it seemed to us less-fortunates that even the principal and the teachers appeared to have special smiles, more intimate notes of cordiality in their voices when they spoke to men who had made the team, but there was a sartorial element involved: those big blue sweaters with the giant "C" across the chest.

Letter Men!

I weighed about 104 pounds in shoes, suit and cap, but

I tried for everything. At first call for practice I was out taking my turn at bat, or being buffeted about in football scrimmage, or trying to toss the ball through the ring on our basketball court. I never made it. It wouldn't be accurate to say I didn't quite make it. I just didn't make it at all. Not even the second team. Not even a bid to become a substitute. It wasn't only weight. Let's face it, I didn't have the stuff.

After a time I did cut a fancy figure on the dance floor, thanks to Professor Rick's instructions, and I soared to the dizzy heights of chairman of the Dramatic Club and Business Manager of the *Argus*, but none of these social achievements entitled me to wear the coveted "C."

And then Lady Luck stepped in and struck a blow in my behalf. At the close of the baseball season in our junior year, elections were conducted for both Captain and Manager of the team for the following term. By some miracle, my name was presented as candidate for manager, one of six in the race. It had something to do with the thrilling showing I had made as a self-appointed cheerleader. The boys and girls did claim no one could make as much noise and cut up like Sobol when he led them in the song and rah-rah routines.

There came the afternoon of balloting. After the first vote, it was discovered that Jim Nagle and I were in a dead tie, and leading the rest of the field. A third ballot was taken, the others being eliminated, and again it was a tie between Nagle and me. Fellows began to make campaign speeches—a few for me—most of them for Jim. It was pointed out that he was actually a member of the team which I was not, that he was a fine athlete, a swell, all-around good fellow. Someone said he couldn't understand how my name had been suggested in the first place, much less voted upon, except that in his opinion I was the noisiest guy in school, as well as the nosiest. He was quite nasty about it, but also he was the star halfback, with weight not only among the boys, but on his ample bones, too.

Then someone arose and asked out loud why I didn't have the good grace to withdraw. How could I explain to him that I yearned for the privilege of strutting around wearing that big blue sweater with the precious white "C"?

So again a vote was taken and again, in spite of all the campaign speeches, the result was the same—that stubborn tie.

Then Nagle, gentleman as always, good sport and courteous, made a suggestion. Let us toss a coin. That is what we did. A neutral party tossed the silver. I hollered "Heads"—and heads it was.

So there I was, manager of the baseball team! Immediately I rushed to the Waterbury *Republican* office, where I was the high-school reporter (at 5 cents an inch) and wrote a story of the thrilling election, modestly pointing out that the boys had elected me, forgetting to add that a toss of the coin actually had decided the appointment. The story appeared with my picture, and it swelled my week's clipping string by eight inches or forty cents.

I think you ought to know that that season we captured the state high school baseball championship and some people—jealous, no doubt—insisted, from the way I told it that I had won the title single-handed.

But there was something I had overlooked.

In those days, only players were entitled to wear the "C"!!

To get back to that championship, the game that decided the title was with our ancient rivals, Naugatuck High. The simple acquisition of the honor was not enough for me. I felt that the occasion called for something more impressive. The result of that impulse, I feel, is adequately described in this ancient clipping from the Waterbury *Republican:*

"A volley of ancient eggs greeted members of the Crosby High School baseball team when they attempted to hold a parade in Naugatuck in celebration of their victory over the Naugatuck team. Louis Sobol, manager of the Crosby team, telephoned to Naugatuck for permission to hold the parade, and it is alleged was told that the Crosby team needed no permit to go through the town. Boro officials said later they did not understand there was to be a parade.

"Chief Schmidt of the Police Department, however, mustered his men as if for a parade and gave instructions not to allow the Crosby celebraters to go through the center of the town. A crowd gathered in the meantime and Captain Malone of the boro force stood, like Horatius at the bridge, at the corner of Main and Maple Streets, and awaited the merrymakers.

"Soon they appeared, Mr. Sobol riding in a touring car illumined with red fire, which was followed by a truck containing a crowd of cheering Waterbury fans. The cavalcade was routed here and there by the police and the crowd followed. Finally Mr. Sobol appeared at Police Headquarters for the permit, only to be told it was unavailable. He was escorted back to the touring car.

"Chief Schmidt, in the meantime, had remained in his office and was informed of the progress of the enemy. On their way home, the Waterburians were encountered near Main Street by the defeated Naugatuck players and their friends. The battle of eggs followed. The local lads departed in omelet formation after they had thrown out of their truck a casket which they had intended to burn on a funeral pyre in celebration of their victory."

Even if a fellow couldn't make the basketball, football or baseball team, he still might be in the swing of things and the life of the party if he could carry a tune. I don't recall any of the boys gathering in Mike's barber shop and breaking into harmony, but on many a night the lads assembled at Bauby's Corner or at noon on the high school steps to blend voices in the sweet songs of the day.

I was very much an outsider on such occasions. After several attempts to break into the select circle, offering a rather croaky tenor, I finally took the hint and became a listener rather than a tuneful contributor. Needless to tell, I ate my heart out with envy and at one time contemplated seriously learning to play a guitar or ukelele and even clipped the advertisement offering the complete course in six easy lessons, pay as you learn. Nothing came of that. I played the piano, but I never was quite as deft on the keyboard as some of the other fellows.

I recall that the members of the famous professional quartets who came to our town to appear at Poli's were men of social prestige and standing and excited as much attention when they dropped over to Drescher & Keck's or Hodson's or Mulligan's as modern minstrel men like Bing Crosby and Frank Sinatra do, except, of course, there were no such dizzy outbursts of "ahs" or "ohs" or this silly swooning business.

The notable quartets were The Empire City, The Runaway Four, The Newsboys, The Revelers, The Bison City Quartet, The Avon Comedy Four and The Elm City Four. Usually these consisted of a tenor, an alto, or second tenor, a baritone and a bass. Frequently it was the second tenor who led the singing; he was the one who played straight while the others cut up with clowning. They were always such cards, these wonderful, wonderful and quite lucky gentlemen of the quartets!

Then there were singing teams like Jans and Whalen, Healy and Cross, Van and Schenck, Willie and Eugene Howard, Williams and Walker—oh, there were dozens of them—and it was just about enough to kill a fellow who couldn't carry a tune to think these fine artists had nothing to do but sing and get paid for what was really a pleasure.

I recall some of the songs that were popular with the harmonizers, both on the stage and at Bauby's Corner. We weren't above pulling out all stops on the corny favorites —"Sweet Adeline" and "Way Down upon the Swanee River"—but there were others that kept us tingling: "By the Light of the Silvery Moon," "Cuddle Up a Little Closer," "Dixie," "Down by the Old Mill Stream," "Every Little Bit, Added to What You've Got, Makes Just a Little Bit More," "I Wonder Who's Kissing Her Now," "In the Good Old Summer Time," "Chinatown, My Chinatown," "Rosary," "In the Shade of the Old Apple Tree," "Moonlight Bay." The list is endless.

Whenever a few of us got together anywhere, voices would sing out sweet songs. I have no recollection that the harmony was anything but extraordinarily beautiful.

It may be that such harmony goes on this very day, right here in my big city and your small town, but I have been to many parties at many homes and the guests have included nationally famed citizens and often luminaries from the show world, yet I can't recall a single instance in a dozen years or more when three or four guests would step over to the piano and blend voices.

There have been times, of course, when a patron will remember an old small-town urge and try to sing out loud in a night club as the band begins to play. If he's known, there are tolerant smiles and a gentle plea from the management to desist, but if he's a stranger, the chances are, if he persists, something will be dropped into his potable which in our set is called a "mickey." That—or the bum's rush.

Young Man with a Horn

Only the other day I was reading about the swollen incomes of the young men who lead the nation's bands. It took my breath away. Fellows like Benny Goodman, the Dorsey brothers, Harry James, Louis Prima and others earn from $150,000 to $300,000 annually, as a result of stage appearances, one-nighters, radio, recordings, etc. It has reached the point where a chap is silly to spend years on a classical composition if he can look attractive in neatly tailored clothes and wave a hand or blow a trumpet in front of a group of other fellows. A band leader is the thing, it seems.

It wasn't that way in those earlier days when most of us who idolized the quartet lads and could identify a half dozen of the new makes of automobiles couldn't name more than perhaps two bandleaders. When one of our crowd who could play the piano or violin or drum solemnly announced he was going in for a career as a musician in a band, it was an occasion for much shaking of heads and shoulder shrugging. "There's a fellow with no ambition," was the consensus.

Most of us knew the six men in the orchestra at Poli's on Main Street and they certainly did not indulge in fancy clothes or high living. If they averaged $30 a week each, they were doing well, although the talk was that the leader, Bert Fulton, was good for $50 a week during the season.

Of course, this was before Paul Whiteman and Ted

Lewis and Rudy Vallee set new musical patterns and became major box-office draws. Our town had its pet little orchestras for dances and balls—usually a get-together group under the leadership of a fine violinist or pianist. It wasn't steady work, and most of the musicians labored at other jobs: printing, or in the clock shop, or at the brass mill, or perhaps ran a cigar store.

I can't recollect ever hearing about an instrument known as the saxophone and certainly none of the little orchestras that played around at the dances featured a trumpet. There were vague stories about the oboe, and the impression was that oboe players couldn't remain loyal to their instrument for long without going a trifle wacky. I never met an oboe player, so I don't know what foundation there is for this legend.

Along about our later high-school days, a couple of bands began to gather a reputation around Connecticut. They were headed by two New Haven lads—one was Eddie Wittstein and the other Barney Rapp. Eddie was popular at the Yale proms and Barney was employed for the bigger dances all over the state. But none of the youngsters followed them, pleading for autographs. As a matter of fact, no one in our section thought of approaching celebrities and asking them to sign little pieces of paper. The notables who came to our town were far and few between anyhow.

Movie stars of the silent films were fabulous persons, rarely seen in the flesh. The actors who came, or the concert stars, were in town for a day or two and usually were guests of honor of the Rotary or Chamber of Commerce. No one bothered them for autographs, however. Radio hadn't come in yet.

We began to pay a little more attention to bands when the new-fangled dances had us all going. Turkey trot, Bunny-hug, maxixe, one-step, etc. But no one acquired the distinction that our modern bandleaders gather unto themselves, and there was no extensive poster billing and feature-story glorification. I don't know too much about the figures of the day, but I would say that any young band leader of that period who earned as much as $7,500 to $10,000 a year was someone head and shoulders above his rivals. A closer estimate would be $5,000.

Boys learned to play piano, violin or the wind instruments with no idea of ever becoming professional musicians. It's different now, of course, and some of my best young friends would much rather be in front of a band with a fat radio contract than be President of the United States.

I can't say that I blame them!

Giddap, Napoleon

It was a long time before any of our neighbors owned an automobile and, in fact, only three families boasted horse-and-buggy opulence. One was Dr. Lopez, who lived four doors away from us. Another was Milkman Cutler, who would harness one of his two work nags to a shiny shay on Sundays and holidays. The third horse-drawn vehicle belonged to two elderly spinster ladies believed to be cousins, whose names I forget. In our youthful, jeering intolerance, we referred to them as the Thin Crows.

Every afternoon about 2 o'clock, except when it rained or snowed, the man from the livery stable four blocks away on North Main drove the horse and buggy over to the house where the Thin Crows lived. They would be waiting on the porch, and the ritual, as I recall, never varied.

"Fine day for a drive, ladies," the man from the livery stable would say, hopefully.

The younger-looking cousin, who seemed to be the

dominant member of the pair, would counter stiffly, "Are you sure you fed him?" The livery man would answer, "Oh gosh, yes. You don't get away with not feeding him. He comes beggin' for it."

The woman would say, "Thank you" and turn to the quieter, older cousin.

"Did you forget your handkerchief?" she would ask, and always the other woman shook her head, but never spoke.

For the rest of us, transportation within the city meant the trolley car. To reach out-of-town places, there was the train or the boat. Once or twice a year, the great excitement was the glorious trip to New York on the fine, snug steamer *Richard Peck*. And of course many had bicycles.

We younger ones never indulged in the extravagance of a trolley-car ride unless the weather was forbidding or the distance was a matter of a few miles. It was only when the older folks went visiting that we went by trolley.

Riding on the trolley car wasn't much fun in Winter, even though the kids always made it their business to ask for a transfer whether they needed it or not. The fun was in Summer on the open car. We always hoped it would be crowded, because that would pave the way for one of two exciting diversions. A fellow stood on the side step, holding on and imagining he was a footman clinging to a perilous perch outside the coach which carried the beautiful queen or princess. Or he rode in front with the conductor, and then our hero became a pirate. The scoundrel steering the captured craft was a pilot under duress because there was a gun poking into his ribs and soon he would walk the plank.

Trolley-car rides were great fun, too, in later years, when you and your sweetheart rode back from the dance in Cheshire at midnight with the moon sneaking in and the woodlands on both sides singing hallelujah.

Gradually automobiles began to crowd into our lives. We fellows in high school found pride in being able to name the makes. For a time the envy of the town boys was a restaurant man named George Pandajis, a dudish chap who owned a cream-colored rakish Mercer, cut out at the sides. It boasted the first wire wheels we had ever seen. Also, some extraordinarily beautiful young ladies were to be viewed from time to time sitting proudly by his side as he drove nonchalantly through town, waving democratically to us envious small fry.

Once George Pandajis and Mike Sauchelli, the steeple-jack, had a race. Danny Bowes wrote in the *Republican* that it was the fastest run since Paul Revere's ride. Where-upon Mike called up Bowes and volunteered, for a small side wager, to race this fellow Revere.

One of the town's leading sportsmen who owned race horses and cut quite a figure, Frank Hayes, blossomed out one day with the town's first swagger Pope-Hartford. It was in this sumptuous chariot that a sports writer named Dan Parker had the very first automobile ride of his life —a trip to Meriden. Frank Hayes went off to the pentitentiary later and Dan Parker is now a big-shot sports columnist in New York.

But the flashiest motor conveyance was owned by an eccentric character reputed to be fabulously wealthy and known as Brainstorm Lewis. It was a crimson Oldsmobile, custom-built, and it roared through town, defying speed limits and traffic regulations. Usually, there was a beautiful blonde young woman by the fellow's side, and there were whispers and hints until it was definitely established that the lovely though flamboyant young woman and the eccentric man of millions were truly wed.

One day a glorious-looking belle came to our town to star in our stock company, and we glimpsed our first impressive-looking National. It was a sport roadster, coated with a robin's-egg blue. The star and the car made a glamorous picture rolling through our tree-shaded streets. Occasionally a handsome fellow rode with her. The name of the beautiful lady in the magnificent car was Justine Johnstone and the handsome stranger was the man who married her later, Walter Wanger, the movie producer. Some years ago, they were divorced, and Wanger married Joan Bennett. When I was in Hollywood, I saw both of them step out of a beautiful and expensive car, but, somehow, it couldn't compare with that robin's-egg blue National in which Justine Johnstone cut such a figure.

When the jitneys made their appearance, there was a sermon by one of our ministers who lamented that this indicated the gradual disintegration of our sturdy civilization, for it would lead to a general softening of our moral tissue. This, he insisted, was the forerunner of an excess of comfort.

Why being able to get to your house in a tin lizzie with four other passengers was more destructive to morals than paying that same nickel for a trolley fare is something few of us stopped to analyze. The sermon was a humdinger, with many graphic references to Sodom, Gomorrah, Nineveh and Tyre. The newspaper on which I then worked ran it on Page One with a one-column cut of the clergyman and a three-column cut of the church.

There was also a very fine editorial in which our paper mildly took issue with the distinguished minister and welcomed the progress so clearly indicated by the arrival of the jitney cars.

Then the motor-driven trucks and omnibuses began appearing with more frequency. However, they did not usurp the place in our busy industrial community rightfully maintained by the huge Chase Rolling Mill trucks drawn by six or eight heavy-hooved, ponderous, dappled-gray percherons. They were magnificent animals. There was no grander thrill than to see them occasionally break into a gallop. They convinced you that the tugging of a truck filled with tons of metal was mere pony play.

The Parting of Friends

It was a silent parting.

There were no tears, no exchange of nostalgic reminiscences, no mumbled expression of farewell to hide the emotional pangs of what was destined to be a long separation.

I simply said to the garageman, "Well, I guess you'd better put 'er up for the duration" and left without glancing back.

I never had a pet name for her. Merely "The Car." But I loved her as deeply and as devotedly as those friends of mine who are more demonstrative and have nicknames and diminutives for their own cars, such as the Old Boat, the Jalopy, the Caddy, the Bew, the Pack or the Chryse. There had been scarcely a day in fourteen years that I hadn't seen her and been with her, patted her on the back and, of course, slapped her about a bit.

Once in a while she whimpered and sneezed and choked and screeched. Then I'd take her to good old Doc Mechanic for a look-over, but on the whole she stood up well through the years, and I rarely had cause to complain.

She wasn't quite the same lady who first courted me and won my heart. In the earlier days we knew her as the Big Yellow Marmon, a block long, who was always thirsty. She wouldn't travel more than six or seven miles without looking longingly at the wayside gas pump. She was always under old Doc Mechanic's care and cost me a pretty penny, but I loved her, and among the interesting folks I introduced her to were Texas Guinan, Jimmy Durante, Mark Hellinger, Paul Whiteman, Billy Rose and Flo Ziegfeld—dozens and dozens of pals and gals and even foes.

The Car in those days took us to places long since only little black-and-blue marks in the memory: the Pavilion

Royal out Merrick Road way or to Guinan's roadhouse where Richard Bennett once got up and recited the Lord's Prayer, or out to Woodmansten Inn where Pola Negri would sit gazing rapturously at Russ Columbo singing from the platform.

Then The Car changed slightly, a more sedate lady now, named Graham-Paige, but she was faithful too, and, in fact, caused me less trouble than when she was the Marmon, but I never could quite devote myself to her until she became a Buick. I really fell for her then.

What a time The Car and I had when she was the Bew, as some of my best friends called her behind her spacious, glossy back. We went on our first trip to California and to Florida. We went to Canada. We drove up into the wilds of the Adirondacks. She comforted me when I lost at the races in Saratoga. She sheltered me and saw that I got safely to my folks' home in New Haven one blizzardy night when cars were fainting by the wayside.

When The Car was a Bew she took me to quaint towns I had always dreamed of visiting. Tombstone, Ariz., for instance, now quiet and ghostlike, where men long ago shot each other down in the streets and in saloons and got hanged by the neck until they were dead. Bisbee, which, from the distance, looked like a toy-town propped up slant-wise and ready to fall with one good blow of the breath; to Washington, where J. Edgar Hoover took me through the FBI quarters; to Santa Barbara, where one of the gentlest souls I have ever met, Brother Philip, escorted me through the ancient Santa Barbara Mission; there, in Santa Barbara, I met for the first time Miss Maude Adams.

The Car and I went to San Francisco, and an impetuous young fellow named William Saroyan came to see us and explained why San Francisco was even more exciting than New York. On our way back, The Car took me to picturesque

Carmel, where I didn't see John Steinbeck, although he was there at the time, but I did meet a pretty little lady who owned a restaurant. She told me she was Sade Carr, one of the first of the glorified of the Ziegfeld Follies, a close friend of Anna Held, Fannie Brice, Eddie Cantor and Will Rogers.

Well, at any rate, you can see The Car and I had some times together. Then came a day when she was supplanted by a glittering glamorous butterfly over whom the garage man rubbed a hand lecherously and murmured, "What a beauty this Caddy is!"

The Car was more beautiful now, there was no doubt, than when she was the Sturdy Bew. She had all sorts of gay little ornaments and she sang softly and divinely when we took to the open road. I came to love her finally as much as when she was The Bew and, being somewhat older now and more tolerant and understanding, I treated her more gently and she responded by causing me no trouble at all.

Then came the war and, after some months, orders. One order from the authorities forced me to mascara and paint her lovely large eyes so that her lids seemed to droop slumberously in half-closed fashion. Night and day we were together. I was preparing to spend a little money on her and buy her a new license tag when another order came. Now I knew The Car and I must part.

I didn't see her for three whole years. Then she came back into my life and has been with me since, a little tired now, worn in body and in spirit, but still faithful. There is every hope that we may grow old together.

CHAPTER NINE

Along Came Sex

Sex was not too expensive in our town.

In fact, if you were willing to credit the unsolicited confessions of the Bauby's Corner Casanovas, much of it was gratuitous. We younger hopefuls, hanging around with these jaded sophisticates, heard tales of amatory exploits and anatomical prodigality that inspired a restlessness and lustfulness in urgent need of assuagement.

We yoo-hooed and whistled at the girls as they passed by, but somehow only good aloofish girls with high standards paraded by during these crises and the promiscuous Jezebels who, if you were to believe our street-corner Lotharios, crowded the town, eager to yield at the slightest nod and the hint of an available pallet, managed to keep out of sight.

However, we had two professional *nymphs du pave*. One named Mildred was a slim, blue-eyed fawn with the face of an angel and the trim figure of a corset model. The other was a dumpy, jolly-looking, slightly bow-legged woman of about thirty. This was Minnie.

Undoubtedly, there were others, but Mildred and Minnie were the acknowledged queens of our sidewalk houri, ready to serve anyone who was white, eager and able. Their price was $2 minimum, but Mildred, who boasted a certain amount of pride and dignity, insisted upon a $2 additional bonus if the love-making was to be conducted in the back seat of an automobile.

In all truthfulness I must confess I never had personal and social contact with either lady. Whatever information I possessed concerning them was gathered from others more daring. The consensus was that, though Mildred was the prettier and shapelier, it was Minnie who offered the utmost satisfaction and efficient service.

Occasionally these two indispensable members of the community were picked up by the constabulary, but I cannot remember that either ever served a term in the hoosegow until one night Mildred forgot her dignity and became a bit too gregarious.

Half a hundred or so of the town's gayer blades, their ranks augmented by a few of our hoodlum set, rented a barn on the outskirts of town and tossed an orgiastic brawl during which some of the ancient Dionysian rites were re-enacted.

Mildred, prodded by the whips of hard likker, was soon the center of the boiling orgy. When the police swooped down upon the saturnalia, their eyes popped at what they witnessed. Some of the elder members of the raiding group, good family men, blushed every time they told and re-told what they had seen.

Mildred was given time to put on her clothes and then was taken into custody. She was quite philosophical about the jail sentence, never once protesting over the injustice by which she and a few imported ladies were blamed, but which ignored the participation of an amateur of good family. In fact, that girl's share in the proceedings was completely hushed up, and nobody ever suspected—except everyone in town, her mother and father included.

At any rate, that was the end of Mildred's reign. Thereafter the more conservative Minnie ruled the roost.

Occasionally rumors reached our ears that certain prominent citizens were conducting extra-marital shenanigans with usually unidentified hussies, but these fallen women rarely made their brazen appearance in public in the company of their married swains.

As a rule, the clandestine affairs were carried on out of town, either in New York or in Boston, where the chances for detection were slim.

But every so often, something went wrong. Then the whole town knew, to the embarrassment of the erring neighbor.

There was the case of one of our leading merchants, father of three children, a reputable and wealthy burgher who contributed generously to all charities.

There was no more devoted husband and father, and indeed on the occasion of their twenty-fifth wedding anniversary, all three of our daily newspapers published the picture of the happy couple surrounded by their handsome children. It was such a nice, contented-looking group.

Then came the explosion!

The merchant was arrested in New York and held on a serious charge. He had, it seems, in a frenzy of passion, bitten off part of his mistress's ear and committed general mayhem on her lily-white body. Her agonizing screams of protest had aroused the entire hotel, including two house sleuths. The first thing our townsman knew he was in the clutches of the Law.

Of course, our respectable dailies did not mention the sordid details, but the good, forthright and robust Sunday scandal sheet blazed out the full and exciting revelations with honest candor.

The affair had been of long standing, evidently. The

woman was the wife of a well-known Manhattan attorney. Our hometown merchant and she had been meeting for their love rendezvous on the average of once weekly for several years.

On this occasion, it developed, retiring to their hotel suite with the customary cold bird and bottle, they had neglected the bird and concentrated on the bottle. Our gentle-mannered, meek little business man had been metamorphosed into a roaring, whoring, rip-snortin' lover-man, ready to rip his lady-love apart.

In court, the woman had to testify from a hospital stretcher and was quite bitter about the whole affair. The fellow went up for a term of years. If I recall, the woman's husband forgave her and welcomed her back, but the little merchant's wife immediately pressed suit for divorce.

Get Going, Satan

There came the never-to-be-forgotten night when I was to have my first—my very first experience—with a woman! Not with a street Delilah, but formally, and with dignity, at Martin Dalton's, the town's long-established bordello.

Naturally, I had never admitted to the more blasé members of my set that I was still a virgin. In fact, having reached the adulthood of sixteen, it was my habit to hint quite casually, eschewing outright boasting, that I had lost my head on various occasions, vanquished by the wiles of a junior Thaïs. I was cad enough, too, to vouchsafe a few intimate details, but chivalrous to the point of never volunteering the lady's identity.

The truth was I had reached sixteen with no closer contact with the Forbidden Phases of Life in the Raw than a perusal of a copy of Balzac's *Droll Tales* and avid attention to the stories of conquest offered by my more experienced and bolder comrades.

And then came this night.

Dan's father had granted him permission to take out the new Hupmobile. Four of us were cruising about town when Jim suggested we ride into Naugatuck. Perhaps we could pick up some girls. We drove into the neighboring town in grand style, whistled and yoo-hooed, stopped the auto, hoping a girl would be curious enough to halt. It was a futile quest.

Then it was that Dan, turning to each of us, asked, "Got two bucks?" Each of us was flush that night; each had two bucks or more.

"Let's go to Martin Dalton's," suggested Dan.

Ever since I could remember, I had heard fantastic tales of what went on in the neat-looking red brick house on the hill. There were endless local legends of the amazing beauty, charm and amorous versatility of the resident ladies, the great beneficences of the tight-lipped, sharp-eyed Martin Dalton himself.

One story which had made the rounds of the town was that a governor of a neighboring state, several years before his election, had been a visitor to Dalton's and there became so enamored of a raven-tressed trollop that he had returned every night for a week, and finally, the girl had walked out with him one night. Two days later they were married.

Then there was the tale (probably equally apocryphal) of the beautiful society matron who once a year came to Martin Dalton's, sat around with him and the Madame, ordered champagne for the girls and, occasionally, pretended to be one of them, only to laugh hysterically when she was selected by a patron to go upstairs.

She never did—just laughed and laughed—and, of

course, the frustrated customer would be mighty indignant and wonder what it was all about. Whereupon the Madame would take him aside, placate him and plead with him to select some other girl.

This beautiful society matron (if you are to credit the legend) had been one of Martin's first housegirls. Like the Governor's lady she had fallen in love with a young society blood and married him. Now, just to maintain contact, she came back once a year for auld lang syne.

At any rate, here I was heading for my First Experience, excited, scared, worried.

If I had had the courage I would have suggested we turn back, but I knew I couldn't face the taunts if I explained the reason for my diffidence. And I wasn't so certain I didn't want to go on with the adventure. In fact, the closer we got to the premises, the more excited I became as my imagination began to work itself into a ferment.

Once inside, Dan was quite at home. I sat in a chair in one corner and watched with envy as Dan wise-cracked and took liberties with the ladies. There were five of them free at the time and they looked radiantly beautiful and not at all the painted bedizened creatures I had anticipated. All wore low-cut evening gowns—daringly low cut. Though I tried to stare boldly, I found myself lowering my eyes in confusion and embarrassment. Finally, Dan whispered to one of the girls, a plumpish Venus. I saw her nod her head. Then, to my utter consternation, she rose, walked over to me, sat on my lap, put an arm around me affectionately and whispered seductively, "Honey, aren't we going upstairs?"

After that, what could a fellow do?

I recall very little about that room upstairs except that the predominant color seemed to be a sickly orange and that a huge, untidy bed dominated it. Once again I sought a chair and sat on it. My plumpish friend, still smiling warmly, was out of her gown in a second and stood there *au naturel*, except for stockings and high-heeled slippers.

I hadn't made a move.

"Honey," she purred, "aren't you coming over?" She sat down on the edge of the bed and beckoned.

There was a torch blowing flame up the back of my neck.

Someone was pounding rivets into my heart.

A numbness was creeping up my legs.

The bedside siren was trying to be patient.

"F'gossake," she exclaimed, "don't tell me you never been with a girl before. F'gossake! Oh, no, no! Say, how old are you?"

"Nineteen," I lied.

"Nineteen? And you act like this!"

"Oh," I explained, meekly, "I was just thinking." I started to unlace my shoes.

"How," I asked, a flash of the investigator inspiring me, "did you get into this business?"

The girl looked at me as if I were something that had crawled out of the woodwork.

"Oh, my God!" she said. "Waddaya know?"

I started to fumble with my tie.

"Say," said the girl, a tone of suspicion in her voice. "You got the $2? I collect in advance."

I fished around in my pocket, peeled off two one-dollar bills from a bankroll of six and handed her the money. She folded it and thrust it under a stocking, so that it showed below the knee.

She smiled.

"You're kinda nervous, ain'cha? Nothin' to be nervous about. You sure this ain't the first time? If it is—you

157

gotta do it some time—and little Ruthie'll be nice to you. Please hurry, dearie."

I sat in that chair and stared at her. My fingers were still at my tie. I was frightened. I wanted to get out of that room, away from this woman and this house.

"Look," I stammered. "D'ya mind if we just sit here and kinda talk. I don't feel like doing anything. I just want to talk."

The girl stared at me and shook her head. "Ya ain't queer?" she asked.

I didn't know what she meant by being "queer."

"I just don't feel like it," I persisted.

Slowly she pulled the gown back over her head. She went to the mirror and smoothed out her makeup, patted her hair, lifted her dress, and pulled her stockings up tightly. Then she lit a cigarette, looked at me again, and said, "Look, you don't feel like doing it, and I don't feel like talking. There's nothing we got to say to each other. So I guess we better go downstairs. There'll be more customers."

I said, "Sure, sure."

She had another thought.

"You don't expect me to give ya back the two bucks, hey?"

"No," I hastened to assure her. "Say, don't say anything about—about my not—well—"

"I ain't saying a thing," she promised.

Later as we drove home, Dan, Jim and Ernie each recited in detail their experiences. Then it came to my turn.

"She must be new in the game," I said, with the proper touch of scorn. "Heck, I had her almost bawlin'. She wanted me to stay—for free. Boy, am I tired! Oh boy!"

One Night in Manhattan

New York, I said to myself, is the wickedest city in all the world. Noxious weed, I said, among the gentle lilies of the field. As an honest reporter it was my duty to wade into the quagmires of sin and report thereon.

I traveled down to the Bowery, seeking out furtive figures in crumbling, scabrous buildings, but it was bitter cold and the shadowy thoroughfare was half deserted. Faintly, from the mission house where hungry men were being fed, came the muffled notes of "Lead Kindly Light."

I moved on to Pell Street in Chinatown. My path was blocked by a group of earnest Salvation Army carolers. Undismayed, I pressed on, seeking a clue or guide to the labyrinth of opium dens and fan-tan dives. The faded sign of Sin Fung Long's cellar lured me four steps down into the musty cavern, where a bland Oriental took my hat and coat and another inscrutable Oriental served chicken soup with egg drop and bamboo shoots.

"Drink it hot. It's better that way," murmured the Oriental with a Columbia University diction not at all suggestive of menace.

I left sinister Bowery and sinister Chinatown to drive up to sinister Harlem to a place called Chuck-a-Luck Pete's, where I had heard sin strutted brazenly and beautiful octoroons lured white men to a fate worse than death. A light-colored bartender lazily poured out a tumbler of Scotch and resumed his conversation. I gathered from the fragments that he for one thought the day of Joe Louis was past, that he was getting soft.

There were no octoroons. There was a middle-aged white man and two middle-aged white women, neither of whom was blonde because they were grey. At another table two young white men were trying to convince a young white girl there was no use going elsewhere—this place was as good as any. But she wanted to go back to midtown. She mentioned the Latin Quarter.

I left and walked up Seventh Avenue to 127th street and joined a crowd, mostly Negro, listening to a firebrand Negro orator. He was shouting "You otta come to God. Oh, yes, 'cause God is good. God understands." I went back to where my car was parked and drove back downtown, cutting around to the sinister San Juan section, where the citizens are mostly dark, too, and the tenement houses scarred and bleak. I listened for the shriek that would curdle the blood. I looked for the flash of the knife. My ear waited for the whine of a bullet.

A figure came to me from out of a darkened hallway and my blood chilled.

"Gotta match?" he rasped. I handed him a packet.

"Keep it," I whispered.

"Thanks, mister," he said. He walked away.

I got back into my car and drove to a place in the East Fifties. This, I had heard, was still a speakeasy, one of the last remaining. Sliding panel in the door, grille gates, no admittance unless known. Some awful things had gone on in here, I was told. Would I get in? I got in. The face behind the slot in the door had eyes which knew my face. A boy took my coat and hat. I listened for the click of chips, the smack of dice. I looked for little rooms with closed doors.

There was only the little lobby and the big larger room with a small bar. At one table I recognized the gentleman who wrote detective thrillers, Dashiel Hammett. Against the bar was the brawny bulk of Quentin Reynolds, and with him the editor of a national weekly.

The bartender said, "This Finland against that Roosia is just like another case of David and Gallico," and Reynolds

160

*downed his Scotch and murmured, "Goliath, Jim, Goliath."
So I left and went to the sinister place know as "21."*

*A well-known character, Ted Husing, sat down with me.
He pointed to an elderly woman with large freckles on her
hands and a mink half-wrap around her shoulders. A good-
looking fellow about twenty years younger than the lady
sat gloomily toying with a tumbler of sherry.*

*Husing whispered, "You should have been here about
fifteen minutes ago. She told him off. Boy, how she laced it
into him! I think the Baron's gonna bar both of them after
this. Wonder where that guy'll get his next meal ticket."*

*The woman called for the check. She paid. She tipped the
waiter, closed her purse, rose, and the young man rose, too.
They walked out without a word to each other, the woman
followed by the young man.*

*I went home and read a thrilling mystery story with a
Chicago background.*

CHAPTER TEN

You Meet Such Interesting People

In my junior year at Crosby High, I began to think of a career. I was too snobbish to contemplate going to work in the clock shop where my father had found contentment, if inadequate pay, for many years. Some of my classmates would find places in the rolling mills or enter business with their fathers or become clerks in the stores around town. Many, of course, would go off to the universities and study medicine or law; some were even going in for forestry. A few, among them one of my most prankish buddies, were planning to become priests.

My own ambition, and I had made no secret of it, was to become a newspaperman. Newspapermen, I felt, had power, enjoyed rare privileges, were welcomed everywhere (sic) and in general lead a lazy life (sic, three or four times). Among Crosbyites who enjoyed position in the community because they were reporters were such luminaries as Dan Parker, Dan Bowes, Ben Boyar, Ernie Cohen and one or two others.

I went out of my way to cultivate the friendship of these lucky fellows, hoping they might help me connect in some minor capacity with one of the local newspapers.

One day Ben Boyar suggested I go to see Timothy F. Barry, the managing editor of the morning paper, The Waterbury *Republican*.

"He'll need someone to cover Crosby," Ben said. "I'm graduating and getting a regular beat. Go in, just walk right in on him, and maybe you'll get the job."

Ten minutes later, breathless, I was in the office of Tim Barry.

"Mr. Barry . . . ," I began, firmly.

He looked up startled. "How did you get in here?" he asked.

Before I had the chance to tell him I had simply walked in, he snapped, "Are you in the habit of dropping into offices unannounced? Who let you in?"

I couldn't explain, of course, that this was part of a long-planned aggressive campaign based on my notion of how newspapermen should act—that is to say, bold, brazen, forward, ruthless, undaunted.

"Why—well, I—I thought . . ." I stammered.

Editor Barry was impatient. "Well, let's have it. What do you want?"

"I'd like to be the high-school reporter for the *Republican*."

"High-school reporter? We have one. He's very good —Boyar."

Barry indicated that the interview was concluded.

But I was determined to follow through.

"He's graduating soon, and I thought—maybe . . ."

Barry, now studying some proofs, barked, "It's much too early. Come back round July—August—we'll talk about it then."

"I thought I'd come in now," I persisted, and, hoping to make an impression, added brightly, "The early bird, you know, sir."

"Come back round August," repeated Barry, unimpressed.

As the weeks passed I became more and more unhappy. I had to know. Nothing was as important to me now as to have that job on the *Republican*. I appealed to Boyar to go in to Barry and put in a good word for me. In the meantime, I applied at the Waterbury *American* and also at the *Democrat*, the two evening papers. I was told they had already selected their reporters.

I could stand the uncertainty no longer. Early in June I was back in Barry's office.

"Mr. Barry," I said, without any preliminaries, "about that high-school job . . ."

He scowled. It was quite evident he was annoyed at this second intrusion.

"I thought I told you," he growled, "I didn't want to discuss this until later in the summer."

"Well," I thrust at him, quickly forgetting I had employed the same "slick" approach on the previous occasion, "I figured the early bird usually gets the worm and—"

Barry looked at me—an odd, disquieting expression in his eyes.

"Have you ever heard," he demanded, "that sometimes the worm turns?"

I stared back at him with a sickly grin. I knew my dreams, my future, my glorious hopes were blasted. My bold, forward approach had not been too effective in snaring a newspaper job. I felt miserable as I started to leave.

I was almost out of the office when I heard him ask, "What did you say your name was?"

I turned eagerly, hope springing anew.

"Sobol," I shouted. "Louis Sobol."

"Well, Sobol," said Mr. Barry, "you come back the first week in September and report to Mr. Ebbert—Ralph Ebbert, our city editor. He will explain all the details. Good-bye."

I became a reporter on space rates. Five cents an inch to cover high-school activities, and the tiny sections known as East End, West End, North End and Brooklyn (not to be confused with the borough just across the waters from where I now work on South Street).

A column was twenty-one inches, but I saw it in terms of $1.05 per stretch. Carefully, each Thursday, I pasted up the fragments—the string—and then measured with the ruler. It was not the best training in the world, I know now, for the temptation was to go in for words—many words. A simple church social which should have been dismissed with perhaps two lines was padded into two fat paragraphs. It is embarrassing now, looking back, to learn how colorful the Epworth League's strawberry festival could be, how impressive an Odd Fellows' smoker, how important even the most casual remarks of a minister or chairwoman.

A runaway horse in the East End, a child who had strayed for an hour in the West End, a bonfire in the North End—these became momentous events when a new reporter, working at five cents an inch, recorded them. My city editor, Ralph Ebbert, wasn't too lenient, but somehow I did manage to ramble on, precious inch after inch. Scarcely a week passed that my pay vouchers didn't come to $6 and then, as the months went by, to as high as $15 per week.

I learned the value of pictures. A single column cut was at least three inches in depth; that meant 15 cents.

A group could be two columns four inches down: forty cents; or three columns five inches down: seventy-five cents. A marriage was often worth as much as fifty cents by the time I listed all the names, discussed the ceremony and dwelt not too briefly on the family backgrounds of the chief participants.

One day, Managing Editor Tim Barry came out of his office, spotted me in a corner of the city room typing out my daily neighborhood notes and invited me with a beckoning finger to join him as he went back to his office. The invitational gesture scared the living daylights out of me because those were the days when city editors were tyrants who spoke only to managing editors—and managing editors spoke only to the gods who owned the newspaper.

Mr. Barry forgot to ask me to take a seat. In fact, Mr. Barry forgot me entirely as the telephone rang. For half an hour he engaged in some vague conversation on a dull but current political situation in which our paper with utmost impartiality was taking strictly the Republican side.

I stood there nervous, fidgety, wondering if my daily contributions at five cents an inch were about to be terminated. Finally Tim Barry hung up the phone, fingered a few papers on his desk, then, as if becoming aware of my presence for the first time, spoke these momentous words:

"Louie, would you like to join the staff?"

I became now a full-fledged reporter—salary $10 a week. The honor was great, but it meant a financial loss because by this time I had managed to become so wordy that my weekly vouchers were rarely under $15. At any rate, a staff reporter was privileged to wear the coveted police and fire badge! It was worth the difference.

I was assigned to the police beat. That meant not only stories about all arrests of consequence, but also coverage of the arraignments in city court. In addition, the police reporter wrote the obituaries, made the rounds of the important lodges and also was expected to turn in a minimum of five personals and five one-minute interviews. Also, he might be asked to rewrite some of the rural correspondence or cover a lecture.

In any case, it was a thorough training. Metropolitan newspapers have their specialists. A man may be a reporter or legman, and never write a word of copy. Or he may be an expert rewrite man, never actually covering the story which he weaves so skillfully.

But on a small-town newspaper like the *Republican*, a fellow not only did his own legwork, but he kept his fingers in exercise typing out the story. And there were occasions when, with press hour at hand, I had to write the heads for my story, too.

I began to realize that a good reporter did not have to indulge in excess of words. The city editor's pencil chiseled down column stories to two paragraphs. I began to eliminate flowery adjectives of my own accord. I ignored runaway horses and chafed a bit when assigned to church socials. What had been fun and enterprise at five cents an inch became a job at $10 a week. Actually there were no new thrills until one morning when I picked up the *Republican* and found—oh, precious moment—my name in full by-line over a story on Page 1!!

It was an exciting and eventful life. I was someone apart from my fellow men, a molder of public opinion, an influence in the community.

City Editor Ralph Ebbert deflated some of this conceit. He was brusque, ruthless and omniscient. He saw through all shams, and his scorn withered any attempt to be smart-alecky. To this day I still feel awe of city editors because of my early discipline under Ebbert. But as the years passed the respect I entertained for the man was swelled by a genuine admiration and affection, and no executive under whom I served thereafter ever commanded more of my loyalty.

During my early apprentice days when, in all innocence, I blithely buried Protestants in Catholic cemeteries, reported the "internment" of a "late, lamented" citizen, blandly described a chimney fire as a "holocaust" and insisted on spelling it the First "Babtist" Church, it was Ebbert who curtly set me straight, taught me the difference between "internment" and "interment"—and then pleaded with me to stick to unadorned "burial."

"Use one-syllable words," he urged. "Don't editorialize. Ask questions. Keep asking questions. Don't take it for granted you know what it's all about. If you're going to be a good reporter, you're going to learn from an interview everything there is to learn about the person you're writing about. His age, height, color of eyes, education, personal philosophy, married, single, children, nationality, bald, color of hair, does he squint, is he bass or tenor? A good newspaperman never intrudes his own opinions into his story nor takes sides. He doesn't have a man hung— he knows he should be hanged. Don't be one of those careless writers who split infinitives or scatter adjectives all over your copy. Don't be an O. Henry when you're writing up an Epworth League meeting."

One of my first assignments, I recall, was the annual high-school dance. I had been told to write my copy double space and not to hand in more than a couple of sticks. I wrote four pages of copy about that dance—a full column. I described every one of the eighteen dances, gave the names of the committee in charge and a description of what many of the girls wore. Also I included a few jokes I had heard that night. I handed the copy in to the city desk and went home, very much satisfied with myself. A nice day's work I thought. I had had fun, I had danced, I had not had to pay admission—and I was getting paid for writing about it. What a soft touch!

When I picked up the *Republican* the next morning I did not find my story, though I searched all over page one. Finally I did locate about ninety words on the dance under a single-line caption on the society page. I went up to Ebbert and lodged my protest. He looked up at me and said mildly, "I had to cut it a little."

As the years marched by, I learned not to suffer too agonizingly when my masterpieces were massacred. I learned to tell the high points of the story in the first paragraph. Later a new school of modern editors did not stress the importance of putting your punch into the first few lines, preferred rather to have the stunner at the end. Nevertheless, I think a story should be written so that, when the emergency arises, it may be slashed to the first paragraph, and still tell all that should be told.

Ebbert decided to leave us for a loftier post in New York. Then it was I discovered how genuinely popular this brusque citizen was. At the farewell testimonial dinner, the high and mighty from all over the state assembled and mingled with us lesser fry, the reporters. Everybody who spoke—and most of them did—extolled the virtues of this newspaperman who was now leaving, and I certainly was ready to agree that never had there been a more exemplary gentleman.

I remember that night for one other reason. I was induced to try my first potent potable—a thickish, chocolaty nectar known as an Alexander. I found it deliciously palatable and gulped down three of them in short order. Then things began to happen. First of all I climbed onto a table and made a speech—I, who blushed and stammered or was completely inarticulate whenever three or more persons assembled. Then I became aware during a lucid interval in my fogginess that I was mounted on the bronze horse of the Welton Fountain in the Green and was shouting and spurring him on to victory. How I got off that horse, how I reached home or when, I never did learn. I was a mighty sick fellow the following day, too sick even to go down to the depot with the others to say good-bye to Ebbert.

I have never seen him again.

The bridge is long between my smalltown and bigtown newspaper days, but the far off shores come closer to view as the years crowd down. A gentleman from the *New Yorker* magazine dropped in to see me some time ago and asked whether I knew the genesis of the gossip column. I told him I thought surely it was born newspaper generations ago and cradled in what we used to call the "Personals."

I recalled how Marie Dunn used to gather in her crop every day. There was a time when I sat at the next desk to hers and listened as she telephoned and chattered and asked questions and made notes. The following morning the *Republican* would have column after column of little items: the engagement of the Mulligan girl, the sailing to Bermuda of the Gosses, the tea party at the Chases. Engagement parties, whist gatherings, showers, anniversary get-togethers, scores and scores of one- and two-liners about the people of our town.

But our editor wasn't content with Marie's herculean efforts. Each of us, from cub reporter to star, had this little caution at the bottom of our daily assignment slips: "Personals—5-Must." A fellow might trip up on a city-hall scoop and get away with it, but let him falter in bringing in those five personals and all thunder broke loose from the city desk.

Five a day each was the quota, and when it happened by luck that six or as many as ten of the little personals fell happily into the notebook there was a tug between conscience and cold hard sense. Should we turn in all six or eight, or save the excess over five for the next day?

When the city desk pressed hard and we fell behind in our collection of the little notes, some of us sank low into the quagmire of deceit. We faked them. Harmless fakes—not the kind to break up homes or rupture friendships—but false they were, may the newspaper gods forgive us! Thus it was that one of us recorded that a certain gentleman whose name was in the telephone book was planning to go to London and Paris on a two-months' holiday. The gentleman selected for the trip was a tragic choice. Unknown to the reporter, his name was already on a neat gravestone, for he had passed on more than three months previously.

One of my sources was Tim Dunnigan, a barkeep. Every second week he would report the trip of one Peter Downey to Atlantic City or Asbury Park. The vacations of Peter Downey became a bi-weekly social item, and I, personally, felt that Peter must be quite a person to be able to afford so many vacations. One day Ebbert called me over. "Who," he asked, "is this Peter Downey? Some special pal of yours?"

"No," I explained. "He is a well-known citizen—an influential citizen of the Abrigador." But, as I had reported previously, Ebbert pierced a sham with discomforting speed. I found myself confessing that my source was bartender Tim.

"Go back to your bartender friend and get me more dope on this Downey. I'm beginning to get interested."

"Yes, Mr. Ebbert."

"That's an assignment, remember. Get me his pedigree."

So I went to Tim and broke him down. Yes, there actually was a Peter Downey. But there had been slight exaggerations. Downey had not quite reached Atlantic City or Asbury Park on his "vacations." He had gotten no farther than the city jail. Downey was the Abrigador's best-known drunk.

Marie Dunn's method was safer and more ethical. Even when the little personals were telephoned in, she was not content unless she called back to verify. As the years went by, they had to hire an assistant for Marie, just to take care of the incoming calls, rich with little nuggets of local gossip, tame in the light of present-day daring, but our town was satisfied and the women turned to Marie's page first, before even reading the ads.

As a graduate of the Broadway school of gossip collectors, I can tell you that the current streamlined method is no improvement over Marie Dunn's. The new school drifts from night club to swank restaurant to theatrical opening night, mingling with the folk of the town. Questions are asked and answered; information is solicited and volunteered. In addition, the press agents are self-appointed assistants, collecting the little personals to report to the columnist, and for their reward draw a mention of their clients. But like that certain reporter who sent a dead man on a holiday, these volunteers, in their zeal to fill a quota, sometimes do a little faking, too.

Marie Dunn's method is much the better.

William J. Pape was our publisher. He was a medium-sized, slow-speaking fellow with the slightest suggestion of a stutter. I can never recall seeing him without the short, stubby pipe in his mouth and a soft, battered hat pulled down over his forehead. He had come out of a hamlet in England and become the owner of the *Republican* when it wasn't much shakes of a newspaper either in circulation or as a revenue-yielder. There is no record that at the beginning he tried the methods of some of the big-time New York editors—that is, injecting sensationalism in the news content, headlines, etc. He must have decided conservatism paid handsomer dividends.

But Pape was always a fighter. He fought city administrations when he didn't like the set-up; he pleaded for civic improvements, took raps at a handful of Socialists (this was before we knew much about Communists) and he blasted away at the evil "blind pigs," as we used to call our hideaway saloons which sold grog on Sundays. Withal, the young publisher was a shrewd business man, for the *Republican* began to prosper.

In those early days Bill Pape must have yearned to own a nice, flourishing paper like the afternoon *American*. The *American* was the class paper of the town and carried the heaviest advertising. There was also a peppery little afternoon paper, the *Democrat*, but we who worked on the morning *Republican* knew it was the *American* which irritated Boss Pape. It went along in its own aloof, snooty way, paying very little attention to us upstarts, and that may have gotten under Bill Pape's hide.

So it was startling news even to those who worked for him when one day came the brief announcement that Bill Pape had bought the *American*. I think it was about then that some of us began to feel a bit awed at the genius of this quiet, slow-speaking chap who never seemed to interfere with us.

The next startling move was adding a daily colored comic section to our paper, an event which drew attention even from New York newspapers and a big write-up in *Editor and Publisher*. Pape began to assume a more important role in state newspaper circles and then became a power in the Associated Press and in national publishing.

It wasn't until after I left the *Republican* that my awe of Bill Pape vanished, to be succeeded by a genuine respect, because now I was not too frightened of him and could speak up to him, which I did on several occasions. I learned that this quiet fellow liked poetry and deep-sea fishing, that he was taking a course in dramatic writing at Yale, was interested in the little-theatre movement and that some of those mailed-fist, hammer-and-tongs editorials that created a little stir from time to time around town had actually been written by him.

Of course I did question his astuteness for a long time after he permitted me to leave his staff rather than give me a $2 per week raise.

Some years ago, when I referred to this, I received a genial note from him in which he wrote: "You say you question my astuteness when I let you leave rather than give you a $2 raise. This must have been some other fellow. If I did refuse a $2 raise, it could have been only because (1) I did not have the $2. (2) You were not worth $2 more."

There were some fairly reputable newspapermen making their mark in New York—Irvin Cobb, and Frank Ward O'Malley, to name only two out of a dozen—but my ideal in those early days was a tall, slim, white-haired "journalist"—and I use the term advisedly—named Chris Downey. What I didn't realize at the time was that though Chris was remarkably deft in spinning an oral anecdote, somehow, when he scrawled it down on paper, it didn't quite come off. He could fascinate you by the hour as he sat with you at a favorite rathskeller, Drescher and Keck's, and amiably poured out half a dozen stories over his Muenschner Pshorr Brau and *fromage du brie*.

He was a great reporter but a dull writer, and I can still picture him walking briskly down one of our main streets with his iron hat set on his distinguished unshorn white locks, both pockets of his droopy raglan coat bulging with newspapers, his pince-nez dangling from a black ribbon around his neck, his thinnish shoulders covered with dandruff. And such dignity, such awesome dignity!

As you saluted him, his first challenge was, "Did you read my stuff yesterday?" If your reply was hesitant and apologetic, he'd snap, "How the hell do you expect to be a newspaperman if you don't read me?"

Chris's "stuff" was a column of reminiscent tales entitled "Caught in Passing" which appeared in our Sunday edition. He was the local correspondent for all New York papers, but most of his assignments came from the two *Worlds*—morning and evening. He had a genius for being able to make a case of wife-beating in the Abrigador sound like a rebellion in Ireland when he queried his New York newspapers. In fact, once the *Morning World* ran a front-page feature consisting of one of Downey's explosively provocative queries, the city editors' prompt and eager order—and then Chris' anti-climactic story.

Chris must have been in his sixties when I knew him, but I never met anyone so keen for a scoop, so alert when there was news in the air. There was no other life for old Downey than the uncertain, underpaid, harum-scarum, often heart-breaking existence of the small-town news-paperman. He was a genuinely happy old gentleman.

There was another old-timer, named Jack Walsh, who could rattle off some weird yarns, too. I am not quite sure he and Chris ever got along too amicably and cannot recall that I ever saw them together. Jack kept rattlesnakes in his bedroom as pets. He used to tell how he was bitten by one of them which had coiled around an electric light fixture one night when he went to turn on the light and had touched the surly reptile. "Well, sir, I just cut open that wound, just cut it right open, sir, poured a little whisky on it, then poured a lot into myself—and then I gave that snake a good talking to, you can bet."

My greatest disillusionment came, I think, when I learned that Charles Thompson Burke, who wrote letters to all the local papers solving the troublesome problems of the world, was a timid little elevator man who was as inarticulate as a church mouse when you tried to get him to give voice to his thoughts instead of putting them on paper.

By-Line

One day I received the assignment to interview President William Howard Taft. He was no longer President, but on the assignment blank he was still accorded full titular honors. His son, Charles, was a student in his uncle Horace's famous academy in Watertown, the Taft School, and the former President had come up from New Haven to pay him a visit.

It wasn't until almost 11 o'clock at night that I received word from my source at the Elton Hotel that Mr. Taft had returned and was in his room. I rushed over and finally, after a great deal of pleading, was told I could come up.

I found the genial old man alone, sitting on the edge of his bed in old-fashioned long underwear. Somehow this put me at ease immediately, and it was no longer the high and mighty ex-chief of our great nation but just a good-natured stout man in longies.

Taft had nothing profound to say, perhaps because I had nothing of a profound nature to ask. Would he run for President again some day? He thought not. Was he happy as a professor now in Yale? He was quite happy. Was he going to write his memoirs? He thought not. How did it feel to be an ex-President? He had never given it a thought.

I wrote that story as if it were the discovery of the atomic bomb. I gave it such an important air that even the city desk must have been taken in, because it appeared the following morning under a two-column cut on Page 1 under my by-line.

In recent years, many gentlemen whom I have come to know during the pursuit of my duties have had things happen to them. I will not be too mysterious about this. I mean some of these gentlemen have either been shot, stabbed, ice-picked, cemented or burned to death, or they have been taken into custody by the aggressive Law. Some of them have "fried," as the saying goes, and others have been placed in duress vile for the remainder of their natural lives.

They were pretty tough lads when the going was good and the law lax. Many of them were mild-mannered and pleasant enough in their dealings with laymen, especially with newspapermen, whom they seemed to respect, because as Capone himself once said pontifically, "You got a chance against bullets and knives, but words can get you down."

I met these "college boys" at night clubs and in restaurants, at opening nights, at the Madison Square Garden fights and at baseball games, and though I can't recall ever inviting them to spend an evening at home with me, studying my first editions, nevertheless, I did not run when I encountered any of them in a dark alley, chiefly because I can't recall any of them ever making a face at me.

So that in my time I have met and spoken with and been spoken to by various "late" and merry gentlemen, including Jack "Legs" Diamond, "Pretty" Amberg, Dutch Schultz, Charles "Chink" Sherman and others, but I have no souvenirs by which to remember them—merely a memory or two, and not especially dramatic memories either.

These extensive if not constructive acquaintanceships were accumulated during newspaper days in democratic Manhattan, where a reporter may look at a thug and still eat his tapioca pudding unmolested.

It was different in small-town days.

I don't remember that I ever knew a hoodlum well enough to sit with him, talk with him, greet him at a ball game or prize fight.

We had a few tough guys in our town, but this was before Prohibition, and no one could put a finger precisely on what it was that made tough guys. Occasionally one or another of them would be in city court, haled for an assault charge, but no one whispered that they had a murder or two on their consciences.

There was one young, tough guy who came from the Brooklyn section of our town—a section which started about two miles down the street from East Main. This young hoodlum had served a short term and was now something of a sinister character because of that. I did meet him finally. He came glowering into the city room of the *Republican*, waving a paper. He was directed to me, and now he pushed that paper in my face and shouted at the same time. He had me scared.

Finally I learned what the fuss was about: a younger brother whose name had appeared in the city court records, charged with drunkenness and assault. It was not true, he stormed. He wanted a retraction. Further questioning revealed the mistake was one of identity. It was an older brother, not the younger one that had been arrested. The younger brother, it appeared, was a fine young man, aged seven, second grade in public school. The tough young man got his retraction. I didn't meet another tough young or old guy until I came to New York.

A Night in Court

The ragged Army of Defeat stood before the bar. Shifty-eyed, twitchy, loose-lipped, ranging in age from twenty to sixty. Some stared up at the slight, serious-faced woman in the black magisterial robe, others with conciliatory pleading expressions, still others with the blankness indicative of minds which do not comprehend or do not care to.

I sat with Magistrate Anna Kross at the 54th Street Night Court and surveyed the platoon of thirteen men on trial—not for their lives. Just thirteen men arraigned on the heinous charge of having been discovered sleeping on park benches.

Officer Robb takes the stand. There is something of defiance in his voice. The woman magistrate has been icy in her veiled hint that the cop might better occupy himself than picking up homeless men.

"Just what is the charge?" she has demanded. "Are they vagrants? Have they done something?"

"I see them sleeping on the benches, so I pull them in," explains the harassed officer.

"But on what charge? Did you examine them? Did you talk to them? Have they records? I'm tired of having men like these brought before me with no charges against them. We haven't the facilities for handling them."

"The other judges," mumbles the policeman, "they always send them up for five days or something when I bring them in."

"Yes the other judges—the easy way out. They don't want to bother," accused the woman. "I know—Commissioner Moses wants the parks kept clean, and he's a conscientious man, I suppose—too conscientious—but it's time we all knew the parks were meant for all of us. The air is free and the

grass is free and the park benches are free—to the rich and to the poor alike."

Officer Robb shifts in his seat. It is evident he does not concur. Bums are bums. He is old in the service; he had had his experience with these bench sleepers.

Magistrate Kross faces the prisoners. Have they any money? Have they homes? Have they jobs?

It appears these men are the very salt of the earth. One thin-necked lantern-jawed young gentleman with a purple Easter egg over his left eye is indignant. He has twenty-three cents; he is a seaman; he has a home. Vaguely, when pressed, he locates the "home" somewhere in the Bowery. His name is Calhoun. A Mr. Deutsch has a home—vaguely, too, in the Bowery—seven cents in his pocket.

"Were you asleep on the park bench?"

He grins. "Yes, ma'am, your honor, I just kinda doze off, but I'm sittin' up—not lay'n' down—just kind sittin' up like dozin'." He makes quite a point of having been sitting up.

A tall blondish thinnish-faced elderly prisoner insists upon flashing a blue card. It indicates he is a non-citizen with working papers of some sort. He cannot understand all this nonsense of being arrested for sitting on a park bench.

The woman magistrate is vitriolic. She turns to the reporter. "This is all silly. I'm going to have to let some of these men go; others I'll hold for fingerprinting. We have no facilities here for handling crowds like this. We need a social-service clinic here; we need more assistants. Maybe in that group in front of you are men with long criminal records. Maybe there's a murderer among them. But I have no charge against them—except vagrancy. If they have a home of any sort, if they have change in their pockets, and unless it can be proved they were actually sleeping on the benches, I can't hold them."

There are no serious cases in the court. A tearful Italian

181

mother comes forward. She is plainly bewildered. Her boy is being held on the charge of having stolen a man's suit. The plaintiff, a fat-faced dumpy young man, seems apologetic. His face droops in despair when the Judge paroles the boy in the care of his mother until Tuesday, when further hearing on the charges is to be held.

"What I am going to do?" he wails. "That's my only suit—look. I'm in my shirt now. I ain't got no other suit."

Wearily, the Judge orders that the evidence be restored to the plaintiff with the admonishment that he must appear—in the evidence—for the hearing Tuesday.

The policeman pressing charges against a stocky, sinister-looking Negro lad is ill at ease when he is sworn in. The prisoner has called him names. He repeats the names—certainly nothing that should be heard by a lady—but the lady is a judge and the law is the law.

Another policeman is on the stand now. His prisoner is a baby-faced, light colored boy. "I see the defendant with four other boys. They're pushing girls when they pass. I catch him and I say how would you like it if someone was pushing your mother or sister?"

The baby-faced boy stands with wide-opened eyes.

He confesses to being nineteen. He looks barely fifteen. He insists he wants to be heard.

He knows nothing. Nothing, ma'am. He's just in the park with four other boys and they shove him right into the girls, and the first thing he knows the cop has got him. That wicked-looking knife the cop has shown as evidence—does that belong to him?

Yes. All the boys carry them.

Will he please tell the Court the names of the boys who pushed him? Yes, one is named Jack and the other John. Their last names? No, ma'am, he ain't never known their last names. He don't know nothin'.

182

In the brief interlude between this case and the next, a breathless young man rushes up to the clerk. "Say, excuse me. You got a fellow named Bradley? He's a friend of mine. I hear he's been arrested."

No, no prisoner by the name of Bradley. What was he arrested for?

"I don't know, but I hear he killed someone and they got him for murder, or something."

"That'll be at the homicide court," the clerk advises, and the breathless young man dashes out.

Now we have a well-dressed fellow with a cane and a shabbily attired taxicab driver. The man with the cane has refused to pay the fare. He is ordered to go home, get money and pay the fare.

Now another platoon of derelicts comes up, homeless men found sleeping on sidewalks in the Bowery or in the hallways. The same dreary routine questions and the same routine replies. All have jobs. All have homes. All have money. But their memories are bad. They can't remember their last jobs or their present addresses.

A coffee-colored prisoner admits he's a bad man when he's drunk.

"Are you drunk often?" inquires the Judge.

"Yes, I'm a drinking man. When I drink I do things."

Another prisoner who looks like George McManus' "Jiggs" confesses sheepishly he has been on a terrific binge.

"How are you now?"

"I'm sober's a judge, beggin' your pardon, madame," he offers.

A nice-looking woman comes forward. "I'm his sister," she explains.

"Take him home with you and keep him sober," advises Magistrate Kross.

"*I'll see to that*," snaps the woman, grimly. The "*reformed*" toper follows her out of the courtroom with a broad grin on his good-natured face.

"*You see*," said the Judge, "*it's like that every night. But you should come and sit with me in the woman's court some night. There you'll see cases that'll wring your heart. There's so much we need to improve our whole scheme of justice, to facilitate the handling of cases like these. They appear trivial, but among them sometimes are the potential gangsters, the hardened criminals, the future murderers. When is a judge to know whether he's making a mistake in holding one prisoner and in letting another free?*

"*That colored boy you saw with the face of an angel may be just an innocent mischievous kid or he may have the makings of a gangster. It's a shame to throw him in with these older, hardened men. We haven't even a separate detention cell for the younger boys.*"

Now there is a middle-aged, baldish chap with a face that looks as if it had been put through a coffee grinder only a few minutes previously.

"*Well, Judge,*" he announces, "*here I am again!*"

CHAPTER ELEVEN

The Restless Era

There came a momentous day when a group of us—and the names, as I recall them, might have been Jim Norton, Jim Nugent, Charlie Zack and Cliff Cross—decided that our city editor was no gentleman. Ralph Ebbert had long since gone off to the lush pastures of New York and this incumbent, in our estimation, was in no way his equal.

Our chief indictment against him, believe it or not, was that every night between the hours of ten and midnight, it was suspected he was conducting a clandestine rendezvous with a certain comely matron of our town. We were completely horrified—we purists and Knights of Virtue—because this city editor of ours, a married man, was carrying on extra-maritally.

So one night, Norton called a meeting at Drescher & Keck's, and, over the lager, a series of indictments was drawn up and an ultimatum that was to be presented forthwith to Tim Barry, the managing editor. City Editor must go—or else!

The following morning we stood before Barry while he pleaded with us. "I never heard of anything sillier," he said. "D. is a good newspaperman—he may have some personal faults—but he's efficient, and you'd be surprised how many nice things he's said about you boys. And you, Louie"—he looked at me, mournfully "don't you know what this is? This is a strike. I don't think I have ever heard of reporters striking. You don't want to get mixed up in this."

Norton, our spokesman, spoke up quickly, "We've made up our minds, Mr. Barry. It isn't for more money— or any change in working conditions. We love this paper— but D.—we can't take him."

Nevertheless D. remained, and we walked out.

As Barry had stated, this was probably the first news-paperman's strike in history. By way of observing the solemn event we adjourned to Drescher & Keck's. After a few drinks, Nugent suggested we go to Martin Dalton's, and console ourselves with women.

In the meantime, Barry, and Publisher Pape and City Editor D. and the society editor scrambled about for news, covered the desk, edited the copy. I must say they got out a pretty readable newspaper without our expert assistance. The boys lingered in town for several days—still adamant —and then one by one left for other jobs.

My father and mother were, of course, deeply disap-pointed in me. They saw in this an end to a promising career. When I told them that Cliff Cross had a plan for our future, they weren't too impressed.

Cliff's plan was that since I was five feet four and whip-thin and he six feet five inches in height and almost as wide across the shoulders, perhaps we might appeal to the Keystone people as a comedy team. Those were the days of the Keystone cops and Mabel Normand and the little fellow with the derby and the cane and the awkward shuffle. We were all set to go to New York to seek our fame and fortune in the movies, when through

Fernald's Exchange, then the employment agency for newspapermen, I learned there was an opening in Glens Falls, N. Y., on the *Post-Star*—salary, the enticing sum of $16 weekly!

So off I went to Glens Falls, and four weeks later I was fired and came back to Waterbury, where Tim Barry, having communicated with my folks, brought me back into the *Republican* fold.

As the months went by, I learned that we had been mistaken about City Editor D., had, in fact, done him quite an injustice. But by this time there was a completely new staff on the paper and the strike only an exciting memory.

And then I found myself working in the bigger town of Bridgeport, which was starting to boom as a munitions center. The newspaper was the Bridgeport *Standard* and the fellow I envied most was Al Jackson, a droll, sad-eyed newspaperman who was considered about the smartest writing chap in our neck of the woods, on a par with Dan Parker of Waterbury and Don Marquis of New York.

Jackson was the city editor of the *Standard*, but the reason I envied him wasn't for his dictatorial powers, which amounted to nothing at all because Kip Crudginton, the managing editor, was the real boss in that city room. No, I had the green eye because, in addition to his executive duties, he had a column of his own.

I went out of my way to cultivate his friendship, which in those days was tantamount to a buck private trying to shine up to a colonel. Nevertheless, we did strike up a friendly relationship and one day summoning up what I considered was the height of courage, I asked him point-blank: would he permit me to write his column just for one day?

To my surprise, he put up no protest at all. In fact, now that I look back, it seems to me he jumped at the offer. It was a great moment in my budding career. I was to write a column.

Now the department Jackson conducted wasn't gossipy or informative. Rather it was a cross between what we read today in the sparkling columns of Arthur "Bugs" Baer and H. I. Phillips—witty, satirical and topical. And it was highly popular in our section.

I could scarcely wait until the late hour in the afternoon when everyone had vacated the office. I was eager to transfer my gems of wit and humor to paper. A columnist at last, just like Don Marquis!!

An hour later some of the charm of the situation had vanished. I had worked out a single phrase in that time— a laborious, unfunny, heavy piece of business, it turned out to be. The twilight crept through the broad, dusty windows. I worked on. Night drew on. I plugged away.

Finally, along about 9 o'clock that night, the column at last was complete. I read it over, and I found it very much to my liking. This was clever, original stuff, I thought. This was what people ought to be eager to read.

Most of my super-clever lines concerned the Messrs. Woodrow Wilson and Charles Evans Hughes who were rivals for the office of President—Mr. Wilson, the incumbent, being very reluctant to surrender the job.

Now on the *Standard* we had a fascinating contraption, a simple-looking device, resembling an ordinary typewriter. But when you pressed down the keys, the words appeared not only on the paper in your machine but on a great rolling canvas of paper two flights down in the window of our plant which faced the street. In brief, it is as if while I were writing this very chapter, people on the street, nineteen flights below, could read this even as I was typing it.

A wonderful invention it was, and very popular in those days with the small-town newspapers. I have no doubt some of these machines are still in use in various parts of the country. When you think of it, the famous electric moving sign on the Times Building which keeps flashing the latest news notes is nothing but an outgrowth of this device.

At any rate, the temptation was too great. I wanted immediate reaction. So I sat down at the electric typewriter and began transferring to it some of my "witty" analyses of the candidates. Then I really warmed up, and before I realized it, I was writing an editorial explaining my personal preference for Mr. Wilson.

Unfortunately, my paper was endorsing Mr. Hughes. Unfortunately, too, the publisher, working late downstairs in the business office, saw the crowd gathering in front of the window bulletins. He ran out to ascertain the cause of the excitement.

A few seconds later he came leaping up the stairs, two at a time, burst into the city room just when I was tapping out a brand-new flash philosophy. Without waiting to catch his breath, he fired me!

As I rose, quite discouraged, he said: "For a few minutes there you were a political editor. We have a fine political editor in Mr. Nolan. As a political editor, you are fired. Now I'm hiring you back—as a reporter. Please try to remain one."

After he had gone, I read the column over again. It didn't seem quite as clever or as funny as before. I tore it up. I didn't write another column until many years later.

Incidentally, much as I liked Mr. Wilson, I did not vote for him. They wouldn't let me. I wasn't twenty-one.

One day, Al Jackson said, "Why don't you get wise to yourself, spending all that dough every week, riding home to Waterbury."

Reproachfully, I said, "Heck, I've got to see my folks. You can't blame me for wanting to go home to see the folks and get one of Mama's meals."

Al said, "Sure, but paying out that dough, Louie. Look, get one of these, why don't you?" He showed me a little book with green coupons.

It was the first time I had seen a railroad pass book.

Two weeks later I had my own, good for rides on the New Haven road for any destination in Connecticut. Practically every newspaperman in good standing had one of these railroad books in those days, and plenty of folks who weren't newspapermen managed to snare a passbook for themselves, just as today a lot of people who can't even read newspapers get into the press rows at the fights and carry police cards.

You can't conceive the thrill, unless maybe you're a railroad president and ride free and in style. To be able to walk into a coach, settle back and, when the conductor comes along, hand him that precious little coupon. There was—and is—nothing to surpass that for imbuing a fellow with a sense of his own importance.

However, the day that precious little passbook arrived, eager as I was to ride over to New Haven on the cuff, I didn't because Kip Crudginton assigned me to write a series on the epidemic of infantile paralysis which had struck the state. So I stayed in that night and wrote four pieces about the sinister ailment. I remember how impressed I was with the medical term anterior poliomyelitis. The next day Kip did give me the afternoon off for having turned out the stories, but I wasn't in the mood to use the pass because that morning one of the nicest girls I had ever known died of the polio.

But I used the railroad pass often thereafter, and my sense of self-importance never dwindled, especially when from a corner of an eye I could catch the curious and perhaps envious stare of fellow passengers. The fact that the conductors came to know me by name and stopped to chat with me about momentous affairs of the state and the union didn't deflate my swelling head either.

One day I received a bid from the *Republican* to come back to a better job at more money. Being somewhat homesick, I accepted. Then it was I used that railroad pass for the last time to ride out of Bridgeport. The reason I never got around to using the precious coupons again was because Woodrow Wilson, who had been hinting we were too proud to fight, decided we weren't, and there we were up to our necks in World War I.

And the war having come, I went over to see the old recruiting sergeant in the Post Office building across the way from where I worked. The next day I was on my way to Fort Slocum—and a buck private's uniform.

The Army paid for my fare that day. So there was no sense in using that book. And when the war was over and I was back at my newspaper job, I discovered one of the penalties a people pays for going to war. The time-honored custom of issuing railroad passes to newspapermen had been abandoned!

Every afternoon after the paper had gone to bed, we sat around in the crummy old *Standard* office, and some of us played casino and some of us wrote letters, but Cliff Robarts usually sat near the window shooting out paper clips. Across the street was the Bridgeport *Herald* and occasionally when George Finley came back from the capital in Hartford, he'd sit at the window of his office and shout over to Robarts. The remarks were never too complimentary.

This was late in 1916 and we were getting tired of that war over-seas. Al Jackson, sharp-witted office humorist, would drawl dolefully, "Get yourselves set, guys. We're going to get into the big bang-bang and come home carrying our heads and legs in nice little bundles." Jackson was city editor. So it would be *lèse majesté* for Robarts to shoot a clip at him. Every time Al talked about the war, Cliff would aim the little wires at my ear—and he rarely missed.

Alvin Bucklin, chunky and freckled, said, "Hope it comes. Yes I do. Me, I'm the first to go. I'm a fightin' man from Alabam' and I wanta go to war with a gun on my shoulder."

Robarts would rasp, "Nuts!"

Cliff didn't want to go to war. He wanted no part of war. Cliff had the war all debunked back in 1916.

Bridgeport was booming. Its munition factories couldn't get enough help, and wages were high. The factories were going full blast and the common laborer was earning as high as $60 and $70 a week with overtime, while skilled labor was getting from $50 to as much as $125 a week with overtime.

Bridgeport's crime rate dropped during this feverish era. There were fewer robberies and hold-ups, a sharp decline in knifings and shootings. The city was prosperous, its citizens working and earning good pay. People do not turn to crime when their stomachs are full, their bodies well clothed, their homes heated, and their pockets amply stuffed with spending money.

Cliff said he had half a mind to quit the *Standard* and get himself a job at Remington Arms, where he could knock off the big dough.

"They don't know what they're fighting for, those screwballs," he said. "If I turn out guns for them to kill themselves off, I know what I'm doing it for—for sixty bucks a week, and that'll be all right with me."

Bucklin thought Robarts was putting on an act. He wasn't really that hard-boiled. "Comes a war," he used to jeer, "and you'll be here—Johnny in the line, ready to do your bit."

"Sez you!" sneered Cliff.

"Hell, war ain't bad," said Norman Hall, who had the only waxed mustache in Bridgeport. "It can be fun." Hall wrote poetry and fairly good fiction and often said the only worthwhile job on a newspaper was war correspondent. He had a deep admiration for Richard Harding Davis.

Frank Malone didn't think war was so bad, either. Frank belonged to a cavalry troop in the New Haven National Guard. As the days went on, only Robarts remained the isolationist, the fellow who saw no reason for America to poke its nose into something that he said was none of its business.

Bucklin was beginning to get bitter, throwing out hints that any fellow with guts would go over and join one of the foreign legions. That *Lusitania* business! How could we sit back and take that! A fellow had to be yellow.

Robarts said, "Americans should have kept off the ship. They should have stayed at home."

Well, to repeat, I left the *Standard* to go back to the Waterbury *Republican*. The early months of 1917 paced by and most of us felt we ought to be in it. It was exciting. You'd think we were already in the big scrap the way we hissed pacifists and anything Teutonic.

In fact we began to chafe a bit about that fine, wonderful old war out of which the short-sighted mossbacks in Washington were keeping us. Of course, in those days, nobody had collected photographs of men lying on battlefields with heads blown off and legs hanging from barbed-wire entanglements. The idea of whole cities being bombed never entered the wildest dreams of even the most war-minded. And no stories had yet crept back of men who would never see again and of boys who quivered with what seemed to be the palsy, and which later we began to know as "shell-shock."

When the powers in Washington finally decided there was no reason why we boys over here shouldn't get into the fun, I can remember the excitement in our town. There was a Philharmonic concert in Buckingham Hall. I'll never forget the cheers and yells that exploded when the orchestra played: "O say can you see?" and as if from nowhere there came marching down the center aisle six National Guardsmen, one of them carrying the Flag.

Most of us wanted to join one or the other of the National Guard units, so we could be with our pals, one big happy family when we went over to clean up that little mess, and see the world besides. The Guard was strict in its requirements, and my weight of 118 pounds was considered inadequate. So I went over to Sergeant Williams in the Post Office and got into the Regular Army.

That night I told my mother and father that I had enlisted—and that I was scheduled to leave the following morning for Fort Slocum. Mama cried and Papa said he thought I was too small for soldiering. He started to tell us the story he had told so many, many times—how he had tried to enlist for the Spanish-American War and the accident which had happened to him on the way to enlistment. Somehow his heart didn't seem to be in the telling.

So I went off to the war and it wasn't until late in 1919 that I was back in Bridgeport again. The boys of the old

Standard were scattered, but Al Jackson was back, this time as sports editor of the *Herald*. From him I learned that Norman Hall had distinguished himself over there, and so had lanky Malone.

And dudish, hard-boiled, isolationist Cliff Robarts, what of him?

Hadn't I heard?

Well, Cliff, still squawking that war was the bunk and guys were crazy to have anything to do with it, had been among the first to enlist.

"Wouldn't you know?" I exclaimed. "Have you seen him lately?"

"No," said Jackson, "I haven't. I married his sister, you know."

I offered my belated congratulations and made some weak joke which Al interrupted gently. He said, "Cliff didn't come back. He had his two legs shot away and he died in action!"

That put a chill on our conversation, but gradually we came around to the other boys.

What about bellicose, patriotic Alvin Bucklin? He must have gone great guns in the war.

Well, now, hadn't I heard about Bucklin? Just about the time we entered the war, Alvin had developed gangrene in one of his sturdy legs. They had cut it off at the thigh.

War Episode

We were in Atlanta, forty of us, who had come from various camps in the Southeastern District. We were there because each of us wanted to be a flying man. We had written to Congressmen and influential military friends to spur consideration of our application. Now here we were, ready for examination. If successful, there was to be a three-month training period. At the end of it we would emerge full-fledged fliers with the rank of second lieutenant.

The examining officer, a Captain Carter, delivered a little speech. The war airman, he told us, was a man not only of courage, but of determination, of intuition, of utter fearlessness—and above all, a gentleman. There was more to being an airman than ability to handle the stick and of keeping off the ground. Any soldier selected for the air service, he said, should feel highly honored. There was great individual glory ahead, the opportunity for achievement that would be recognized.

Now we were placed under the guidance of various non-commissioned officers. There was a severe test for the eyes and the ears. There was a thumping and stethescoping of heart and lungs. A civilian fellow tapped our knees. We were told to strip and bend this way and that way, to walk on our toes, then on our heels. Bundles of bright-colored thread were placed on a table. We were asked to determine the colors.

One by one we sat in a chair, not unlike a swivel chair, and twirled about. When the chair stopped we were commanded to look out of the window at the horizontal lines separating the bricks in the walk of the building directly outside. The chair whirl made our heads reel and the lines swayed up and down, first rapidly, then slower, then came to a complete stop. We were to announce promptly when the swaying lines stopped.

Only nine of the group were passed, and I was not one of them. I was not one of them because the examining officer was not convinced I was truthful and therefore eligible to the ranks of gentlemen. He did not consider me truthful because I had stated that I had once as a reporter covered courts.

"A court reporter?" he inquired.

"Yes, sir."

"How fast are you at shorthand?"

"I can't take shorthand."

"A court reporter?" he repeated.

"Yes, sir."

"And you can't take dictation in shorthand?"

I tried to explain that as a newspaper reporter I had covered courts and that it was not essential to know shorthand. It was evident he had confused the assignment with the court reporters appointed by judges, but I couldn't make the difference clear.

At any rate, I was not among the nine who were accepted. But Sergeant Gillis Wilson of Fort Oglethorpe came through with flying colors and I was pleased for him because he had set his heart on being a war flier. We had become friends in our two days together, sharing the same room in the Y.M.C.A. Before I left to return to Fort Caswell, we had promised to write. Neither of us kept that promise.

The war went on and word seeped back of great exploits by flying men of all nations. Raoul Lufberry, Eddie Rickenbacker, Richtofen—others. Thrilling stories of heroic air duels, of chivalry, of death. I kept looking for the name of Gillis Wilson among the cabled stories, but there never was mention of him.

I met Wilson again in 1929, while covering an English show, *Bird in Hand*. There he was, pushing with the rest of us, in the lobby during the intermission, and he recognized me first, but didn't quite remember my name. He was fat now and slightly bald, and he had the manner of, and looked like, a successful salesman. He told me he was operating a large and prosperous grocery store in Upstate New York.

He and his wife sat with me in the old *Graphic* office while I wrote my review (I was drama critic then), and later we went uptown to a speakeasy. There, over our drinks, I learned what had happened to Gillis Wilson.

He had served his training period and had been one of the few in his class to be awarded a commission as first lieutenant. For six weeks, after he landed in France, he had participated in no action. Then one day, he and three others ran smack into five German planes. In the battle two of the Americans were dropped and he and the other flier were forced down behind the German lines, both their planes and their bodies, safe and sound.

It was humiliating, and he felt he never wanted to come out alive and have to face the other fellows and admit he had come down unscratched. And that, he confessed, was all the fighting he ever did in the Great War.

The airman who forced him down and made him prisoner was friendly—and even sympathetic. Gillis told me his name, and I did not think of it again until World War II exploded. Then I remembered that the name of the sympathetic German flier was Goering—Hermann Goering.

Rube Wardell, the general manager of our syndicate, needed little urging to reveal how he had "sold" the eccentric realty millionaire, "Daddy" Browning.

"I said, 'Look, Mr. Browning. This is it. Your name and that lovely little lady's—and your pictures, Mr. Browning— this big! Get that. This big—right across this whole double-truck!' Know what I mean by a double-truck? Now, here is one page, a single page. Cost maybe a thousand—fifteen hundred, maybe two thousand dollars—for a single day's advertisement. But a double-truck, Mr. Browning, that's the whole business—the two pages in the center spread. Two pages, and all yours for free, your name, 'Peaches' name, your pictures, and a wonderful story, day in and day out, signed by you and by 'Peaches.'

"That got him! I had him, especially when I spread out those two pages and waved my hand over them to show him the size of the letters his name would be in."

When I came to work for Famous Features Syndicate the "Daddy" and "Peaches" Browning first-person series had already been launched, appearing both in the flamboyant Evening Graphic *and in the* New York Journal, *as well as in some fifty or sixty newspapers throughout the country.*

Editor Leslie Fulenwider, a tight-lipped, cruel-eyed, good-looking young fellow told me I was to draw $75 a week to assist Don Garden write the first-person stories for the Brownings. Although I already knew the story, he insisted upon telling it to me in detail. How the publicity-mad sixty-year-old millionaire had courted the buxom, good-looking Frances Heenan, known as "Peaches"; how he and Wardell, in order to promote the sale of the series, had devised a succession of stunts—one of them the "disappear-

ance" of the sixteen-year-old bride, and later her "recovery." I was not to ignore the mysterious acid burns which had scarred "Peaches" lovely face and her legs, but always to keep it a mystery.

So I pitched in and became "Peaches" and "Daddy" and laughed myself sick when I saw the elaborate Page One stories which either Don Garden or I had written. I had other duties. Queen Marie of Rumania was a client, and when her letters failed to arrive in time, I sat down and wrote them for her, under her by-line. Helen Keller, the blind and mute genius, was another whose writings we peddled, but it was very seldom that I had to rewrite her offerings.

We were a "ghosting" outfit. Even while I was still patching up in print quarrels between the Brownings or plunging into flamboyant and maudlin confessions of love under the by-line of either "Daddy" or "Peaches," I found myself assigned to assume several other identities. Thus I became pretty Charlotte Mills, whose mother, the attractive choir singer, had been discovered murdered with her sweetheart, Pastor Hall, under a crab-apple tree in Lovers' Lane in New Jersey. One day I was even James Mills, her mild-mannered Papa. On another occasion, I found myself writing under the name of Natacha Rambova, who once had been Mrs. Rudolph Valentino.

Naturally, ever since my "ghosting" days I have been more than skeptical whenever I read a sprightly piece by a tennis champion or a pugilistic monarch or an aviator or a comedian. I can understand why Mr. Jack Dempsey, for instance, might operate a restaurant successfully, but if tomorrow a novel should appear, bearing his name as the author, I would sulk in disbelieving rebellion from Bowling Green to Van Cortland Park.

When the beautiful Queen Marie came to New York, the city made a royal fuss about her. Naturally, since I had been her "alter ego" so many times, I expected to meet her and visit with her for a long and intimate chat. When I suggested I should meet the noble lady for the sake of good old Famous Features, my boss, Fulenwider, regarded me coldly and snapped, "I think not, Sobol. Not Queen Marie."

I never quite understood just what he meant by this enigmatic but definite slough-off, but later concluded that Fulenwider did not consider me dignified enough a representative of his firm. In fact, he made it plain that I was too plebeian to come within the royal presence. I must write in her first person singular, but I must not presume to look upon the Queen.

Another transference of personality occurred when I became the Gibbs Siamese twins, recounting "our" various difficulties, "our" pleasures, "our" confusions and "our" hopes. One day, even, I was their mother, suffering all the travail of the parent giving birth to infants doomed to be joined together for life, and I had to do a great deal of vicarious worrying about their future.

Of course, nothing I ever "ghosted" will dominate our national archives, but I seem to recall that one crisp, cryptic line inserted in one of "Peaches" Browning's effusions resulted in a dramatic composograph in the now defunct tabloid, the Evening Graphic, in which the now equally defunct "Daddy" Browning was revealed on his creaky, elderly knees, holding up the mask of a dog's head while over his well-corseted figure was spread a bear rug. The balloon floating from "Daddy's" mouth revealed him barking, "Woof, Woof" at the naive, plump and precocious "Peaches."

"Daddy" came running into the office, and spread the picture out on Wardell's desk.

"Nice, very nice," he conceded, somewhat stiffly. And then hesitantly he added, "Ah-er—well, now—I wonder, though, is it quite dignified?"

CHAPTER TWELVE

═══════

Yes, Some Days Were Happy

The Army let me go one blizzardy day in February and I came back to the small town and my newspaper job. I came back with a great warmth and affection for the old neighborhood and a determination never to stray too far away again. I was twenty-one. I had a job, and most of my friends had returned from the war, uninjured. Life was good and promising in this little city which still maintained many customs dating back to Colonial days, including a pole in the Green on which all court orders as well as summons notices were posted.

Our skyscraper was nine stories high, and its only rival was the tall clock tower of the quaint railroad station. The truth was we didn't go in for buildings with their noses in the clouds. Ours were low and unpretentious but snug and warm, like our citizens. An inland town, we boasted a wisp of a river which even at flood-tide rarely commanded enough water to cover the rocks which cluttered the river bed like so many bald-heads thrust out from bedcovers.

There were no thickets of forest lands, and the mansions were few and not too pretentious. Certainly I have seen more impressive business centers than East Main and Bank and South Main, but nowhere kindlier-looking churches with such grace and charm to them that the impulse to enter and be at peace with yourself and your God was irresistible.

The war over, life again became serene and uneventful. We met in Exchange Place in the early hours after supper and watched the pretty girls go by and blushed a bit if among them, by accident or otherwise, was our own pet. Nights were calm and the heavens above bluish-black and every star shone clear and low, so that you felt you could reach up and pick them out one by one, like bulbs out of an electric sign. Night life came to an abrupt close about 10 o'clock, but the more daring among us stayed out much later and congregated at Mulligan's or Hodson's or the Chinese joint, where if the chop suey wasn't so good, it was at least plentiful for the 30 cents you paid, which included all the tea you could drink plus rice cakes.

If you were one of the select few who worked on the local morning newspaper, you stayed out even later, of course. You came to work at four in the afternoon and you quit at three in the morning (unless yours was the 2 P.M. to midnight shift). Those post-midnight hours were spent usually at the squalid little police station, where Desk Sergeant Jack Cavanaugh told tall tales of hunting exploits —both man and beast. There came an eventful day when the new City Hall was dedicated, with its brand-new police station. Now the desk sergeant was a lieutenant and he no longer thrust his stockinged feet against a pot-bellied stove. Having achieved dignity, he no longer condescended to tell tall tales. But you waited around, nevertheless, while they brought in the drunks or the brawlers and occasionally the painted ladies from one or the other of the two bordellos.

And if the fire alarm rang, you rushed over to the fire headquarters and rode with the chief to the scene of the blaze, trying not to appear too important. These fires rarely amounted to anything, but occasionally, as in the case of the Connecticut Hotel disaster, you came face-to with death leaping from the flaming windows.

At twenty-one I became a city editor—rather, to be quite truthful, an acting city editor, for the boss was a bit dubious about handing all that power over to a youngster fresh out of the Army. Twenty-four dollars a week they paid me, and now I could distribute the free passes to the movies and the vaudeville and burlesque houses.

From 6 P.M. to 3 A.M. I sat at that desk and handed out assignments to the staff, okayed expense accounts, made up Page One, argued with the foreman of the composing room and then ran back and barked at the one office boy. It was gay.

There came a night to try any young inexperienced city editor's soul. With the forms locked up, ready to go on the presses, every light in the plant went out. We phoned frantically and discovered the entire city was in darkness. Something had gone amiss with the city's power plant. The darkness didn't worry us. What did send us into a panic was that this was press hour and our presses were dead. I sent two reporters over to the fire headquarters with instructions to bring back lanterns. They returned with a dozen, and we had light.

The phone rang. Two children had been killed by a trolley car—a brother and sister. The accident had happened at 11 o'clock. Death came at 2 A.M. By the dim, flickering light of a lantern, a reporter tapped off two sticks on what ordinarily would have been the most important story of the day for a small-town paper.

The police reporter rushed in. An important figure of

the city's sporting fraternity had been stabbed by a woman. He was dying. The reporter wrote out a dozen lines for a Page-One box.

And then to cap the climax, a fire broke out in the heart of town—Exchange Place. As it developed, it didn't amount to much, but at the time we had no way of telling how serious it would be. Another boxed story covered that.

Up in the composing room, the linotype machines silent, the foreman and his assistant set the three stories by hand in the semi-darkness. We forgot deadlines. At 4 o'clock power was restored, the presses rumbled, the papers came tumbling out with the queerest makeup in their history.

Next day I awaited eagerly the word of appreciation from the managing editor—to whom naturally I had made full written report—with no pretense of modesty over my efficient handling of the situation. There came back a sharp note from him, calling attention to a violation of the paper's rule book in the wording of one of the emergency heads!

Yes, life was good in a small town when a fellow was just past twenty-one—and worked on a newspaper. There was Drescher & Keck's or George Mulligan's or Hodson's where the boys gathered for ale and small talk. There was Lake Quassapaug on a Sunday afternoon or Shells Hitchcock, to dance with your best girl in her pink organdie frock and the ribbon around her seventeen-year-old blonde head. There was the lake to canoe her around in, and even a carousel. At twenty-one I wasn't ashamed to ride on a merry-go-round, although my head spinned whirl-dizzy.

There were penny-ante poker games after hours in the office, the fights in the Armory on Friday nights, baseball games in the afternoon. A newspaperman was friendly with the cop on the beat and the high and mighty lieutenants, captains and even superintendent. He called the postmaster by his first name. Why not? Hadn't he once been a newspaperman himself? Sometimes the big stars came to town in shows and the young Greeley went over and sat with them in their dressing rooms.

There was a time when, in addition to his other duties, he was also the sports editor. Golf was a game of mystery to him, but as sports editor and, in fact, the entire sports staff, it was his duty to cover the tournament at the Country Club. He followed the formidable gentlemen around, completely mystified. Finally, after the tourney was over, he threw himself on the mercies of someone named Walter Hagen. Mr. Hagen dictated the story. The young sports editor wrote it almost word for word as he had gotten it from Mr. Hagen.

To his bewilderment, the story was the sensation of town, at least among the country-club set. Calls came in, asking for the name of the new humorist. Folks had never read anything funnier, they insisted. They wanted more of this type of humor on the stuffy sports page. Mr. Hagen had played me dirt. He had handed me a line of double-talk in which he had incorporated every sports term out of lacrosse, hockey, water polo and soccer, mixed them up into an olla podrida, and spiced the stew with a few confused golfing expressions to give it all a taste of verisimilitude.

As sports editor of a morning paper, it rested with me to give decisions in important fights—at the time ours was strictly a no-decision state—and whatever the man covering the event for the morning paper wrote was the word that went out over the wires.

There was a fight scheduled between a fighter named Dummy Martin (he was a deaf mute) and the middle-weight champion, Al McCoy, derisively referred to as the "cheese champ." On the afternoon preceding the night of the fight, a dapper gent came into the office and asked for me.

He seemed a trifle dismayed to be facing a thin, undersized youngster, but he recovered quickly and came to the point. Briefly, if I would see my way clear to declaring Martin the winner in my report on the fight, he would see his way clear to making it worth my while.

I rose to my full five feet four of righteous indignation and told him to get the hell out of the office. He was a blot on the landscape. Trying to bribe a newspaperman!!

All the remainder of the day I sizzled, and Dummy Martin had two strikes against him in my book when he left the stool in his corner of the ring to meet the champ that night. But the truth is the truth. Martin literally made mincemeat of McCoy. He won every round easily. The champion was practically out on his feet at the end of the fight.

Under the circumstances, although without too much enthusiasm, I had to report faithfully that Martin had beaten McCoy.

The following day when I came into the office, there was in my mail box an envelope which had been delivered by hand. Out of it floated two $1 bills and a note. The note was from Martin's manager. It read: "Thanks, kid, I knew you'd see it my way."

I must skip a few years to another episode in my rather mild early newspaper career. It was my day off and, together with one of the reporters, I was riding in a battered Ford up around Woodbury way when the breeze wafted something in our direction that wasn't the aroma of autumn leaves or the perfume of hillside flowers.

As we drove on, the hideous odor seemed to be closer

and sharper. Jim said, "That smells like something dead. Wanna know something? That could be a dead guy."

A second later we spotted through a clump of bushes on this isolated country road what appeared to be a hand sticking out of the brush. We climbed out of the flivver and investigated. By newspaperman's luck we had stumbled upon the decomposed body of a taxicab driver who had been missing for ten days.

A young man had eloped with a girl and dropped out of sight with her. When last seen, they had been entering a cab. The cab had never returned. The police hinted at foul play.

And now we had come upon the body of the missing driver. We drove five miles back to the nearest farmhouse, borrowed a small Brownie which had some unused film in it, snapped pictures of the murdered man and rushed back to the city.

It was a mighty exciting story for a small-town newspaper, and even the Associated Press picked it up. In the meantime, I telephoned to a news-picture service in New York and asked whether it wanted to buy the picture. Back came the reply: "Yes. Come to New York with the film."

I took the afternoon train, and all the way up enjoyed visions of walking into this news service's office with the picture and story and so impressing the editor with my enterprise that he would hire me on the spot.

Unfortunately, by the time I reached that office in New York, it was after ten at night and only a subordinate was there. He told me to leave the picture but return the following morning, when I would be paid. I roamed Broadway and the side arteries that night, mingling with the crowds and a great hunger arose in me to become part of this exciting metropolis. To be a reporter on a big

New York newspaper. I made up my mind, some day, somehow, I was going to work in New York.

That night I stayed over in a cheap hotel, and the following morning I went down to the office of the news-picture service. To my disappointment, the editor didn't come out to see me or leave instructions with the girl at the reception desk to have me come in and see him. Instead, she directed me to a cashier where I filled out a slip and was handed $40 to cover all expenses, plus payment for the picture.

The picture and the story were never used because that day something far more important dominated the news-papers. Death had come suddenly to President Harding!

I forgot the girl in the pink organdie and the ribbon around her hair when a red-haired beauty in a plaid skirt came to town for a day. She was a friend of Ben Boyar, the same Ben who had paved the way for me to become a reporter and who was now an important figure in the New York theatrical world. She was eighteen and her hair was spun sunset, I thought, and her smile was out of a Swinburne ode. It was Spring. So we went to Justice Fred Bauby. I remember what he said as we stood before him.

"Beautiful day, isn't it? Nothing like a Spring day. What's on your mind?"

I said, "I thought maybe you would like to marry us."

Justice Bauby looked out of the window, then looked back at us and said, "Now isn't that a coincidence? I was just thinking when you two came in that perhaps you would like to get married because it is Spring."

So he married us and I gave him $2. Half an hour later the heavens opened and deluged the city, but there was Spring in my heart and in the heart of the red-haired girl, I guess, for we stepped out into the rain and walked and walked until we reached Hamilton Park, where a solitary deer ran back and forth in a wired enclosure.

My bride left me that night to go home and tell her papa and I telephoned and told my mother and father. Then I went back to the office and tried to fit heads on copy, but finally had to give it up. So I went off to a corner typewriter, and all that night I wrote poetry. It was not good as poetry, but there was lots of it.

A week later, my bride came back to town to join me.

I said, "I get $24 a week over at the *Republican*. That isn't enough for two people, is it?"

"Isn't it?" she asked, vaguely.

"No. In New York, men on newspapers earn $50, they earn $100—more."

"They do?"

I said, "I've saved $110."

"Isn't that wonderful?" purred my bride.

"Know what I've decided to do? I'm quitting. We're going to New York."

My wife said, "Yes, dear."

That was all so very, very long ago. You must get me to tell you what happened to us thereafter.